JOYFUL UNCERTAINTY

God instructs the heart not by ideas,
but by pains and contradictions.

Jean Pierre de Caussade

JOYFUL UNCERTAINTY

Roy Williamson

First published in Great Britain in 1999 by
Triangle
Society for Promoting Christian Knowledge
Holy Trinity Church
Marylebone Road
London NW1 4DU

Unless otherwise stated Bible references are from The New Revised Standard Version of the Bible © 1989.

British Library Cataloguing-in-Publication Data

A catalogue record for this book is available from the British Library

ISBN 0-281-05248-4

Typeset by Pioneer Associates, Perthshire
Printed in Great Britain by
Caledonian International, Glasgow

Contents

Introduction 1

1 Private faces in public places 5

2 Am I free to be me? 22

3 God is great – pity about the church 34

4 Jesus is Lord – but not always 50

5 Believing with your fingers crossed 64

6 Brass heavens 79

7 Where is God when it hurts? 94

8 Walking the edge holding the centre 109

References 122

To
all who joined me on my pastoral walks, especially Andrew Nunn, James Bogle and Malcolm Goldsmith, my constant companions on the way, and to Helen, Jean, Anne and Paul, who 'looked after the shop' while I was on the road.

I am grateful to my editor Alison Barr for her patience and practical advice, to my long-standing friend Rob Marshall for his encouragement and to Leslie Morley and Jonathan Williamson for reading the text and offering suggestions for improvement.

Introduction

The story is true. The first thing I did when I was made a bishop in the Church of God was buy a pair of walking boots. Cope and mitre, ring and crozier are customarily considered as essential episcopal gear but to them I added walking boots – and have never regretted it. From the outset I was determined not to be desk-bound nor to be over-protected by episcopal outriders but to get out and about alongside people in their local communities. A pair of walking boots was essential equipment if I was to walk through the Yorkshire dales in the Diocese of Bradford and, later, along the course of the hidden rivers of south London and around the edge of the Diocese of Southwark.

Over 14 years the same pair of boots has carried me across fields and farms, up hills and down dales, through leafy lanes in east Surrey and West Yorkshire and along concrete pavements in Bermondsey and Blackfriars. More importantly they have brought me into one-to-one contact with thousands of ordinary, yet extra-ordinary, people and rewarded me with life-enriching insights into the ways and works of God in their daily lives. I rarely, if ever, returned from a day's walk without my missionary resolve renewed and my heart warmed through listening to and sharing in the stories of others. Invariably I received more than I was able to give.

I also discovered that people are more ready to open up in conversation with a person walking alongside them on their own home ground than they are when playing away from home in a more formal religious setting. I also experienced, in common with those who walked and talked with me, a touching honesty and a refreshing absence of superficiality. Somehow, with all the trappings of religion absent, so also were all attempts at pretence. A few were clearly trying to impress, but the vast majority welcomed the opportunity to chat naturally in an open and relaxed manner – though the steep terrain of the Yorkshire dales and the hustle and bustle of a Brixton market sometimes made that difficult.

What became increasingly clear during these personal encounters was that people were often struggling with the so-called contradictions of life. In other words, they were living, successfully or unsuccessfully, courageously or despairingly, with those apparent inconsistencies of life in general, and religious life in particular, which often confuse and confound our belief and behaviour. Such contradictions or inconsistencies are universally experienced. We find them within society, within the church, within ourselves and, some would claim, even within God. It is not easy to live in a society where all are made in the image of God but some are disdainfully pushed to the margins. Nor is it comfortable to live in a church where prejudice and stereotyping still frustrate the mission of God. Sometimes it is difficult to live with yourself when your heart tells you to do one thing and religious prudence tells you to do another, and it can be frustrating to follow a God of revelation who sometimes hides himself.

On my travels I became more aware of how people deal with the contradictions of life. Some have the capacity to accept them without question – whatever will be will be. Others simply ignore them and, with a sunny disposition, concentrate on the positive things of life. Many people struggle with them, either triumphing over them or being depressed by them. Some are angry, more are puzzled, and several have given up practising the faith because of them.

The further I walked and the more I listened the greater became my conviction that here was an area of common human concern that was worth reflecting upon in the hope that I might learn to live more confidently and courageously with contradictions and, perhaps, help others to do the same.

So this simple book came to birth. To claim that it is of God would be arrogant in the extreme. To declare that it is all my own work could dissuade the discerning from reading any further. To believe, as I do, that the compulsion to write it came from God, lays no blame for its shortcomings at his door, but at mine. It also may illustrate one further contradiction, namely, that an infallible God should commit one aspect of his cause into the hands of a very fallible human being!

The chapters that follow try to get to grips with some of the challenges of living with contradictions. They are written, hopefully, to encourage and inspire ordinary people on their journey in or towards faith. Their purpose is to help people see that many of the frustrations, anxieties and doubts they experience, though painful and perplexing on occasion, are, nevertheless, a necessary part of life in an imperfect world and in a church which is not yet what it is called to be.

When the author of Psalm 23 wrote:

> He makes me to lie down in green pastures;
> he leads me beside still waters;
> he restores my soul.
> He leads me in right paths
> for his name's sake.
>
> (Psalm 23.2–3)

he was absolutely right, but so also was the hymn writer, L. M. Willis, when she penned these words:

> Not for ever in green pastures
> Do we ask our way to be;
> But the steep and rugged pathway
> May we tread rejoicingly.
>
> (L. M. Willis, 1864)

The underlying conviction of this book is that contradictions are essential raw material for growth to maturity as persons and as Christians though, as the following chapters will indicate, it can be a difficult process.

I have altered, of course, the names and locations of the various people mentioned in order to preserve their identity.

I

Private faces in public places

Will he be wearing a purple cassock or blue jeans?

I am told, on good authority, that that was the question which filled the minds of those people, from the different parishes, who awaited my arrival each day in order to walk with me along the next stage of my journey through my diocese. To put it another way, they were saying to each other, Will he be dressed like one of 'us' or like one of 'them'?

For most, it was simply a matter of curiosity. They had never walked through the streets with a bishop before so they didn't know what to expect. For a few, the question was posed with some anxiety. It had taken enough courage to volunteer to accompany the bishop in the first instance, without having the added embarrassment of meeting your friends while walking alongside someone in fancy dress!

For me the matter was never in doubt, though I have been told that one or two were disappointed that I turned up in blue jeans – even though a wooden pectoral cross, a clerical collar and a real shepherd's staff gave the game away. It was never intended to be a solemn ecclesiastical procession but a purposeful walk, during which I would listen to, and encourage, those I met on the way.

But the fact that the question was being asked and the matter discussed pinpointed, in a simple and somewhat humorous way, the dilemma which, perhaps, all people have in integrating their private and public lives. It is a dilemma so succinctly highlighted by the well-known poet W. H. Auden in his famous phrase 'private faces in public places' (Auden, 1932).

It is a challenge faced not just by church and political leaders nor, for instance, by those who have been given a high-profile status in business, sport or broadcasting – though the pressures upon all such people may be particularly intense. No, the dilemma, which so often requires us to live with contradictions, is common to most people. Some have to cope with the contradictions in the glare of media publicity. Others wrestle with them in the shadows of anonymity. Dave was in the latter category.

Unrealistic expectations

He had an attractive personality. He was intelligent and articulate – and he was willing. In other words he was just the kind of person many churches grab hold of for 'up front' ministry. His local vicar was not slow in making use of his talents, and who could blame him. Isn't that what so-called 'every member ministry' is all about? But in Dave's case there was a downside, and he shared it with me as we walked.

He was having a crisis of integrity and it had all to do with unrealistic expectations. Being so frequently in the public eye, reading lessons, leading prayers and, among other things, directing stewardship in the church, had led to an unhelpful presumption on the part of others. He was being perceived as a person of great spiritual maturity and people, including the vicar, were beginning to look to him for the kind of help he couldn't provide. The assurance with which he performed up front was not matched by a similar assurance when it came to matters of faith. He certainly wasn't an unbeliever. He was happy to throw in his lot with the local church and give what help he could. He just didn't have the level of Christian maturity that others were attributing to him and he felt bad about it. Living with the contradiction of not being the kind of person which, apparently, his public stance declared him to be, made him feel hypocritical. No one else in the church was aware of his dilemma, but it was getting to him and he needed to share it with someone. The only way he could live with this contradiction was to share it.

Strangely enough, that's exactly what Tom and Barbara said to me as we walked across an open stretch of moorland. 'Please, can we share something personal with you? We need to talk to someone about it and we think you might be the best person.' Their dilemma was not dissimilar to Dave's but rather more intense. They were being perceived as so-called backsliders – those whose faith had 'gone off the boil'.

Before moving to their present church some months ago they had been very heavily involved in the life of their former local church. They had run the youth group, hosted Bible studies in their home, edited the parish magazine and were members of the pastoral care team. They were considered to be key members of the congregation. Needless to say the vicar was sorry to lose them when Tom's job necessitated a move to another part of the country. However, he did the decent thing. He wrote to the vicar of the parish where Tom and Barbara were going to live. He painted them in glowing colours, informing the minister concerned how fortunate he was to be receiving two such tireless and committed workers.

The new vicar's expectations were high. Tom and Barbara were just what he needed. There were several gaps to be filled in the work of the local church and he couldn't wait to welcome the couple with open arms. But he got a shock. For weeks they never turned up in church and when they did, they hurried off quickly after the service, not joining in the customary coffee and chat at the back of the church. They were not only feeling embarrassed about all this, they were also feeling a little guilty about failing to meet the expectations of the vicar and other members of the church.

As we talked, however, it became apparent that their change of lifestyle regarding involvement in their local church was the result of humility, a desire to be real rather than false. They had been exhausted and overwhelmed by their level of commitment in the previous church. Some of it had been by their own choice but much had been foisted upon them. They had been on a treadmill, and they had found it impossible to get off without letting people down. And, like Dave, they were aware of and oversensitive about the gap between what their public work in the church declared them to be and what they knew themselves to be – not spiritual giants but struggling disciples. They didn't wish to be exposed again to such contradiction without first having a period for rest and reflection.

How wise they were. And how sensitive the local church became in the months that followed. They were offered appropriate pastoral care in which they were given space, and valued for who they were, rather than what they did for the church. It resulted in a renewed and healthy commitment within the local congregation.

I use the phrase 'healthy commitment' because there is another and more chronic form of the same contradiction which I encountered more than once on my walks and have witnessed far too often in my ministry. It sometimes leads to physical burn-out, marriage breakdown and loss of faith. It relates to an unbalanced commitment which results in too much time being spent in doing what is considered to be God's work in the church and too little time being spent on the immediate needs of the family and home. It starts with the best of intentions but imperceptibly becomes all-consuming, so that relationships within the family are damaged, sometimes beyond repair.

The pastors of the church need to be sensitive in nurturing their flock. Willing people must not be overloaded, however capable they may appear to be.

Unrealistic expectations must not be allowed to cause unhelpful contradictions between our private and public lives. I speak from personal experience.

Thrown in at the deep end

I shall never forget that dark, wet, February evening in 1978 when I returned home from Southwell Minster where, without even a modicum of formal training, I had just been installed as Archdeacon of Nottingham. As I turned the key in the lock of the door of my home I heard the telephone ringing. It was just inside the front door so I didn't even get my coat off before answering it. Picking up the receiver I was still too new and too shy to say, 'Archdeacon of Nottingham here'. But I needn't have worried. The vicar on the other end wasn't listening. He just wanted to say one sentence – 'Now that you're an archdeacon I have a problem for you.' As a one-hour-old archdeacon I was expected to be a fount of archidiaconal wisdom, knowledge and experience. The expectation was flattering – but somewhat unrealistic. The immediate challenge facing me was, do I confess to being ignorant or make a pretence of competence? Was there a middle way? Could I, with a touch of Irish blarney, so confuse him with a multitude of words as to make him wish he hadn't posed the problem in the first place. I opted for honesty and said, 'I don't immediately have the answer to your problem but I will find one and ring you back.' Still wearing my coat I made straight for the study and the volume entitled *Halsbury's Ecclesiastical Laws* and discovered the answer. I rang him back immediately, feeling quite pleased with myself, only to be told that the vicar was busy and couldn't come to the phone right now!

It was a reasonably light-hearted beginning to a new ministry but, as many of my readers will know, there is a serious side to it. Unrealistic expectations are the cause of very many personal disasters among those who are thrust from the realm of the private person into the role of public leader. The high casualty rate among football managers, for instance, is not only an interesting statistic, it is also very often a total disgrace. But it usually springs from unrealistic expectations and, as such, is not limited to the world of sport or, indeed, politics. As my encounters with Dave, Tom and Barbara, and other couples revealed, you will find it in Christian churches up and down the country.

It comes into particularly sharp focus among those charged with the responsibility to choose suitable ministers for their parish church. They tend to go head-hunting for the Archangel Gabriel, only married. It is perfectly natural to look for the best person for the job but it is both dangerous and unfair to create expectations that are so impossible to fulfil that even the Archangel Gabriel would fall at the first fence. I have seen too many godly and sincere ministers broken and sacrificed on the altar of unrealistic expectations, and it could so easily have happened to me.

Make or break

Written indelibly on my memory and, I think, seared

into my soul, are some words from a leading lay person of a parish in which I served as a fairly young vicar. With a sense of pride, he said, as I began my ministry, 'This parish will make or break you.' I couldn't quite believe what I was hearing. I think there was meant to be a compliment in there somewhere, for the parish was a tough one and others before me had encountered real problems. But his words came out as callous and insensitive. They spoke of expectations and did so in fairly brutal terms. In essence they declared that depending on my public performance as vicar of their parish my personal reputation and my future prospects were at stake. No mention was made of me as a private person, the husband of one wife and the father of five children, with all the God-given responsibilities that involved. No mention was made of me being called by God to do his work in that parish. It presented the classic contradiction in terms of success or failure. It was a far cry from the Man of Nazareth who said, 'I am among you as one who serves.'

But it wasn't all that far from the wilderness temptations where personal reputation and popular success were very high on Satan's agenda, but Jesus preferred to follow the way of the servant of God. Apparently only two possible futures awaited me – promotion or brokenness – and we know which of those reflected the spirituality of Jesus. For Jesus the way of the servant of God was the way of integrity, the way of hiddenness, the way of being true to God which risks failure.

Human expectation needs to make allowance for human vulnerability, personality and temperament.

The ways of God, as revealed in Scripture, make clear that he chooses the weak as well as the strong to do his work. He can work through their failure as well as through their success. He uses the introvert as well as the extrovert in the work of his kingdom.

Sometimes the situation calls for an aggressive attitude and temperament, like that of Simon Peter. At other times it requires a gentle, somewhat mystical, personality like John the Apostle. And who can doubt that the complex, energetic character of St Paul was just right for his missionary task in the early church? God has a place for all types and temperaments. And he has a place for failure as well as success, though I wonder sometimes if, unlike us, he even thinks in such terms. Nevertheless, there is an unhealthy attitude around both in society and in the church regarding success. In society it appears to be the only thing that matters. Failure is the stock-in-trade of the 'no hoper'. In some areas of the church success and prosperity are considered to be signs of God's blessing. Failure, on the other hand, especially if it is identified with falling numbers and struggling congregations, is equated with either lack of faith or, to use modern jargon, losing the plot.

I dare say Jesus might have been accused of the latter. He was by any rational standards a fool and a failure. Though God, as it were, had invested everything in him he ended up as an object of derision and contempt at a public execution. Yet we know that what looked like failure turned out to be God's way of fulfilling his purposes for humanity and the whole of creation. Besides, the resurrection of Jesus plainly declares that failure is never the last word.

Honesty the best policy

As I said in my introduction, one of the features of walking alongside people on their own territory was their readiness to be open and frank with me. That was certainly the case with Dave, Tom and Barbara and many others I shall mention during the course of this book. It was a great privilege to be on the receiving end of such honesty. I, in response, was honest with them and noted their sense of relief and encouragement as they discovered that some of their personal struggles were similar to mine.

That was no surprise to me. Among them were teachers, doctors, nurses, social workers, company directors, farmers, journalists, policemen, accountants and a host of other professional and non-professional people, all of whom were wrestling with the inner contradictions of being 'private faces in public places'. Many of them were working in situations where moral dilemmas, for instance, did not present themselves in black and white but, inconveniently, in various shades of grey. Often the choice confronting them was not between good and evil but the lesser of two evils. Indeed, many of them were facing new challenges and problems for which there were no pre-packaged answers. Trial and error, patience and understanding, courage and uncertainty, together with the ever-present need for public accountability, was a day-to-day reality for most of them. The prudence of the public person may have required one thing, but often the personal principles of the private person longed for the opposite.

Clearly, that was no forum in which to pretend that I was free of such contradictions, that I was so integrated a person as to be above and beyond all that. It would have been dishonest and lacking in integrity to do so. Again, honesty seemed the best policy and, pastorally, the most helpful. So I shared a little of my story with them.

How, on several occasions, I had stood at the back of a long procession of church dignitaries about to enter the cathedral for some great service and found myself whispering, 'Lord, what am I doing here?' For better or worse I was perceived as a professional Christian. Deep down in my heart, however, I was only too well aware that I was still very much an amateur. Still a learner, always the disciple who follows. Here was I, called to lead, teach and inspire many who were more able, better qualified and holier than I. The public person was dressed for the part and by the grace of God could, to use modern parlance, 'do the business', but it meant living with the ambiguity of my own inner uncertainties and the expectations, some of them grossly unrealistic, of those whom I served. There were times when I felt like an impostor and was glad, therefore, to recall those mysterious words from Corinthians, 'We are the impostors who have to speak the truth, the unknown men whom all men know' (2 Corinthians 6.8).

Commentators vary in their interpretation of these words. To me, however, and to people like Dave and

Tom and Barbara and to many others who are called to positions of major leadership, they reflect a little of the contradictions experienced by private people who find themselves thrust into public ministry. We are called to proclaim truths with a certainty we don't always feel. To admit doubt or even suggest that you are struggling with an element of the truth can lay you open to a charge of unsoundness or unfaithfulness. Because of our public position we are known by all, and what we say, especially if it is controversial, will be heard by all. Yet we know that if we were out from under the trappings of leadership no one would take a blind bit of notice either of who we were or what we said.

Whatever the true interpretations of these words from 2 Corinthians, few commentators would disagree that they highlight one of the major themes of the letter, namely, the reputation of Paul. His reputation was at stake. His opponents were accusing him of double-dealing. But in the face of such suspicions Paul asserts his utter transparency and openness and his single-minded commitment to his vocation as sent by God. The glory of God, over and above his personal reputation, was the controlling motivation for his ministry to the Corinthians and the vision which sustained him as he lived with contradictions. His policy was one of openness and honesty before God.

Talk to any Christian leader who is prepared to be open and frank and they will tell you of the gap that so often exists between their public roles and their private struggles. The danger comes when they are not prepared to be honest about it. Disaster threatens when they insist on clinging to the top of the pedestal for dear life, afraid to come down lest their halo should slip and the private person be seen. When that happens, then all too easily the public face swallows up the private person. The latter disappears and is totally replaced by a sort of pompous, public figure who is always pronouncing, supremely confident, never owning up to feebleness or failure.

How important it is in such circumstances for someone to come alongside us and help us to get ourselves and our situation into proper perspective. 'Come off it', is not exactly a biblical saying but it is certainly a biblical sentiment addressed to those who are taking themselves and the contradictions of life too seriously. Humility is a vital ingredient if we are to have any success in living with contradictions when other people or the system would turn us into the kind of people we don't wish to be. A sense of humour doesn't go amiss either.

Humour and humility

When Harold Macmillan, who had been Chancellor of the Exchequer under Anthony Eden, became Prime Minister in the wake of the Suez débâcle, he received a personal letter from President Eisenhower which began, 'Dear Harold', and welcomed him to 'New Headaches'. He wrote: 'I assure you that the new ones will be to the old ones like a broken leg is to a scratched finger. The only real fun you will have is to see just how far you can keep going with everybody chopping you with every conceivable kind of weapon . . . remember the old adage, "Now abideth faith, hope and charity – and greater than these is a sense of humour"' (Horne, 1989, p. 9).

President Eisenhower's theology may have been slightly awry but his instincts on the need for humour were spot on, as I discovered in the early days of my episcopacy in Bradford. At the end of a confirmation service I was confronted by a lively and fairly strident octogenarian who informed me that he had worshipped in that church, man and boy, for over 70 years. But not only was he blessed with such longevity, he also had a retentive memory, for he told me in no uncertain terms that nothing of significance had happened in the Diocese of Bradford either before or since the episcopate of Dr Donald Coggan. I swallowed hard and, searching for deep reservoirs of charity and grace, congratulated him for his long life and faithfulness, agreed with his estimate of Donald Coggan, and shook him warmly by the hand – only to receive the immediate reaction, 'Oh! Dr Coggan's got a bigger hand than you!' I almost choked with laughter.

But the point is an important one. Unless we are able to laugh at ourselves and encourage others to laugh with us the likelihood is that we will take ourselves too seriously. And it is when we do that that the contradictions become almost impossible to live with and, all too quickly, we lose our joy and sense of proportion. Jürgen Moltmann, the German Lutheran theologian, had a particularly perceptive view of laughter. He wrote, 'I have an idea that laughter is able to mediate between the infinite magnitude of our tasks and the limitation of our strength' (Ward and Wild, 1997, p. 286). I am convinced that Moltmann is right. The contradiction between what God sometimes calls us to do, and the total inadequacy of our own strength for the task, leaves us with two alternatives, despair or laughter. Despair comes when we take our eyes off God and are left only with our own feebleness to contemplate. Laughter comes when we recognize that God knows all about our weakness, and we wait with joyful, even hilarious, expectation to see how he is going to use that weakness to fulfil his purpose.

Small wonder that George MacDonald, the Scottish poet and pastor, said, 'It is the heart that is not yet sure of its God that is afraid to laugh in his presence' (Ward and Wild, 1997, p. 180). I believe that laughter comes from God. Indeed, I would want to add a further sentiment to that of George MacDonald, namely, it is those who are unsure of their relationship to God who are afraid to laugh at themselves.

That sentiment is not as way-out as it may first appear. It was uncertainty about their relationship to God, and to each other, that made the disciples so miserable and ungracious on the night Jesus washed their feet. On their way to the upper room they had had an argument as to which of them was the greatest. Clearly, in the impending shadow of the cross they needed a lesson in humility, and they got one. They had been so preoccupied with status, it seems, that they ignored the common courtesies of washing the feet before supper. So after the meal Jesus rose from the table, wrapped a towel around himself, took a basin of water and, kneeling on the floor, proceeded to wash the dirt from their feet. He was unfazed at putting himself in a servile position where others, if they had a mind to do so, could look down on him with contempt.

Jesus was not concerned about status. He was sure of his relationship to God – he had come from God and was going to God. And he was sure of his relationship to them – he had come to save them, a fact dramatically and prophetically demonstrated in the act of foot-washing. That left him free to serve them in the way he did, not only in washing their feet but in all that was symbolized by that washing.

The point to grasp is that in Jesus dignity and humility walk hand in hand. They are not mutually exclusive. That speaks volumes to the matter that has been before us in this chapter. It would be short-sighted to imagine that Jesus was exempt from the contradictions experienced by 'private faces in public places'. How then would we account for his tears, in Bethany at the grave of Lazarus, over Jerusalem at the time of his visitation, and in Gethsemane on the eve of his death? How also would we explain his sensitive concern for his mother, 'Woman, here is your son. Son, here is your mother' (John 19.26, 27), at the very moment when he was engaged in a gigantic cosmic struggle with the powers of darkness? Far from being exempt from contradictions he experienced the contradiction of human existence intensified by his affinity to God.

Jesus is unique. He was a victim of unrealistic expectations who was destroyed by the system, yet he triumphed over them both. His love for God, his Father, and his love for people gave him a singleness of purpose that could not be frustrated by contradictions. Yes, Jesus is unique but he is also our exemplar. We are to learn from him. We are to grow in love for God and each other so that the inevitable tensions and contradictions of being 'private faces in public places' will serve to fulfil rather than frustrate the work he calls us to do.

2

Am I free to be me?

Most husbands and wives play games. Anne and I are no exception. When she adopts a particular attitude towards me I often tease her by saying, 'Oh, but you remind me of your mother.' She is not slow to return the compliment when need requires, 'And you're just like your father!' Behind the innocent and amusing banter, however, there is a serious question to be asked. And Susan asked it.

Along with several others we were sharing a picnic during one of my pastoral walks. It was half-term and several young people had come on the walk. Susan's two young teenagers had come with her. My simple remark, that they were very like their mother, was meant as a compliment, but it sparked off a major discussion that lasted for two or three miles of the journey after lunch.

Susan's upbringing had not been a happy one. She had been somewhat damaged by the experience and was anxious lest she in her turn should adversely influence her own children. Most parents have shared that particular concern at one time or another. For Susan, however, it was symptomatic of a deeper anxiety regarding a contradiction which existed within herself as a person and which impinged upon her faith. Though she felt herself to be in charge of her own life, there were times when she was aware that inherited traits and external influences also determined the kind of person she was. Indeed, she felt they sometimes made her the kind of person she didn't want to be, and left her confused as to just who was in control of her life.

It was some comfort for her to discover that she was not alone, that others shared the same experience and asked the same question, though perhaps in a different way. Nevertheless, she was struggling with the contradiction of trying to be herself and, at the same time, feeling that past influences and present pressures were frustrating her freedom to be so.

Susan's question was, 'Am I free to be me?' She smiled as she asked it but I was left in no doubt that it represented a serious concern not only for her as a person but also as a mother with two teenagers, each of whom would quite likely be asking a similar question as they progressed through their adolescent years.

It's a question that needs confronting and it comes in a variety of unexpected forms; none more challenging than the frequent exhortation to 'be yourself', whatever that may mean.

Be yourself

How often have we offered that advice to others? It trips

off the tongue so easily. I've said it to my children as they have faced new and demanding tasks. I have said it to myself, again and again, as I have started a new job and become aware of the unrealistic expectations that others were determined to foist upon me. And how often have I tried to follow my own advice – with only partial success? What does it mean to be yourself? Is it possible to be yourself or must we live with a degree of contradiction?

One of the couples who journeyed with me during a pastoral walk in the Yorkshire dales reminded me of something I had said to them on the day, a few years before, when I had conducted their wedding service. I had pictured each of them carrying a large suitcase as they stood side by side at the front of the church waiting for the solemn words that pronounced them man and wife. The imaginary suitcases, I had said, were packed with all the luggage that they brought with them from their past life. The suitcases were full of the historical, psychological, emotional, spiritual, professional, social and cultural building blocks which, over the years, they had acquired from their family and friends and from their various experiences of sadness, joy, failure, success, love and hope. These were the things that had made them the kind of persons they were. This was the raw material out of which their new life together would be formed, for better or for worse.

I think the image is a valid one. Each of us does carry luggage from the past. Many of us have memories of events that have shaped our lives for good or ill. 'If only' is a longing concept that all too frequently haunts us in our moments of depression when we are pondering how things might have been. Most people are aware, for instance, of the way parental influence shapes our lives. Most are also aware of being 'messed up' to some extent by failures and dissatisfactions in personal relationships from childhood on. The idea that we still carry around with us the child that we once were, and that his or her problems still affect our lives in subconscious ways, is a powerful one that rings true for many people. The popular knowledge of psychology and genetics, and the widespread debate about the break-up of traditional family structures, have increased the awareness of the importance of parental and family influence.

Sometimes, of course, an unhealthy preoccupation with such things produces a negative reaction: 'I am only this way because my parents, society, genes, made me so; it's not my fault and I can't do anything about it.'

It's not my fault

I sometimes wonder if the prodigal son ever said such a thing to those who may have criticized him for leaving home and wasting both his life and his inheritance. The story in Luke 15 never ceases to be a fruitful field for reflection and, perhaps, speculation. I know, of course, that there are deeper truths and wider implications underlying this famous story told by Jesus but I have little doubt that the basic elements of it reflect a domestic reality in the experience of many. Did the younger son feel unable to be himself while he stayed at home? Was the influence of his father and older brother so constricting that he just had to make a bid for freedom? And, crucially, having done so, was he free? Was he more truly himself?

The remainder of the story suggests that he was not. He clearly was not free from the inbuilt personality weaknesses that caused him to waste his life and his inheritance in such a shameful way. He certainly was not free from the selfish influence of his new-found friends who, when he was in dire straits, refused to help but, rather, took advantage of him. Thankfully, he also found that he was not free from the memories of the caring concern of his father and the comforts of home. They haunted him in the far country. They drew him back home. And, as we shall see, they led to a discovery of true freedom and his real self. In this connection the Authorized Version of the Bible has an interesting description of the moment when his fortunes changed, declaring that 'he came to himself'!

But the one thing that is absent from the story is any suggestion that he had got into the mess through someone else's fault. That, somehow, he couldn't help himself. That he was the victim of external circumstances. That others were to blame.

It is true, and Susan's anxiety was based very much upon this fact, that we are born into a network of relationships in family and society which suffer from shortcomings and imperfections. To some extent they are bound to fail and mess us up from time to time. But it is also true, as the Christian faith claims, that there are deeper roots to this condition than mere family relationships. These roots lie in humanity's estrangement from God. They lie also, perhaps as illustrated by the prodigal son, in a natural self-centredness which inhibits our relationship with God and with others.

Yet, despite these predetermined handicaps and constraints, the Christian faith insists that within their limitations we are still able to make real choices, to make the best or the worst of what we have got.

As Susan and I walked and talked it became clear that despite the handicap and constraints of her past experience she had made choices that had given positive and creative shape to her life and brought lasting benefits to herself and her family. Like most other parents she had made her mistakes but, as she admitted with justifiable pride, there was evidence for all to see that she had made the very best of the building blocks she'd been given.

I am loved

But it wasn't just a case of making the best of what she'd got. She felt there was more to it than that and, as she shared her experiences, it became clear that she was already finding the answer to her own question. She was discovering that in a very special way she was loved and valued by God.

Like many others, she had suffered for years from a lack of self-worth. Those who work with young people, for instance, are only too well aware of the problem. All too often the façade of arrogance, rebellion and truculence that young people appear to have is simply a smokescreen to hide an inferiority complex. Underneath there is a crisis of self-worth. Their peers are better, prettier, cleverer than they are. Life seems to have conspired to leave them in the starting blocks while others got off to a flying start.

That was Susan's experience. And she had carried some of that luggage with her into adulthood. She was always putting herself down. Always afraid that when others discovered her real self she would be rejected. But her reintroduction into the life of the local church and the sensitive and understanding pastoral care of her minister had brought about a change. There was taking place a gradual but sure realization and acceptance of the fact that she was loved by God, as she was with all her anxieties and contradictions. This was resulting not only in an increased and altogether healthy love for herself, but also an enriched relationship with other people, including the members of her own family.

Though the circumstances were totally different, Susan's experience of discovering that she was loved was not so far removed from that of the prodigal son. The awareness of being loved made the difference. Of course, we might cynically believe that it was an empty belly that brought a change of heart to the young man, and we may well be right. However, I prefer to believe that it was the memory of a caring and loving father that was the prime motivation for his return. And it was the powerful, understanding and non-judgemental love of the father's welcome that set him free to be his true self. He came in penitence, asking for forgiveness from God and from his father. He was willing to return on reduced terms, as it were, prepared to forgo his former status in the household and ready to fetch and carry like a hired servant.

But it wasn't to be. Love refused to allow him to be less than his true self. Love said to him, 'Be yourself'. He was his father's son. So, despite his willingness to become a servant, the love of his father required him to be what he was, a son in his father's household. He always was loved, of course, even before he left home, but it took the experience of the far country to make him appreciate it fully and to realize where his true freedom lay. It was the realization that he was loved, always was and always would be, that set him free to be himself, his true self.

Who will set me free?

The trouble is that when people are struggling with the same question or wrestling with a similar dilemma to Susan's, they imagine that they are alone. That somehow such things don't touch other people, that the strong are not afflicted with such frailties. They are wrong. Even a person of the spiritual and intellectual calibre of St Paul experienced contradiction and conflict, within his own person, as to the controlling influences upon his life.

He gives us a graphic insight into his personal struggle in his letter to the Romans (7.14–25). There was a fight going on within his person between his old nature, empowered by sin, and his new nature, empowered by God's Spirit. The conflict produced a confusing dilemma to such an extent that he said, 'I don't understand my own actions'. Instead of doing the things he wanted to do he found himself impelled to do the very things he hated. 'I can will what is right, but I cannot do it', he said.

Paul was experiencing the contradiction that all Christians have to live with, namely, our old nature in sin and our new nature in Christ desiring different, even opposing, things. So, for instance, my Christian mind will take great delight in proclaiming the person and work of Jesus Christ but, at the same time, my selfish nature may be engaged in self-promotion. The desire to be recognized as a good preacher may, inadvertently, overshadow our presentation of Jesus as a wonderful Saviour. Those who have exercised any leadership in the church will acknowledge the pertinence of what I am saying and the reality and power of the temptation to which I refer. All of us, if we are honest, will admit to the conflict within us and the contradiction we live with as a result.

Paul was honest. That's why two apparently contradictory cries were wrung from his lips. One was a cry of despair – 'Wretched man that I am! Who will rescue me from this body of death?' The other was a cry of triumph – 'Thanks be to God through Jesus Christ our Lord!' This man, out of his great spiritual maturity, acknowledges his need to be delivered from the power of his sinful nature, which he likens to a corpse strapped to his back, 'Who will set me free from this body of death?' And, with both honesty and assurance he answers his own question '. . . Jesus Christ our Lord'.

It is not without significance that it was the overwhelming conviction that God loved him that transformed his life and set him free as a person to fulfil his apostolic ministry to the glory of God. He said, 'the Son of God who loved me and gave himself for me' (Galatians 2.20). As we read the letters and observe the life and work of this somewhat complex character it is clear that he just couldn't get over the wonder of the love of God for him. The matter of personal identity and freedom to be his true self was resolved in the love of God for him. As with the prodigal son, that love had been looking and searching for him, even when he was unaware of it. Despite his past follies and failures it embraced him as a child of God and gave him his identity (see Acts 9). Jesus, whom he had persecuted, became the very one who set him free, for 'if the Son makes you free, you will be free indeed' (John 8.36).

When and how?

The Susans of this world are fairly pragmatic. They may be impressed with stories of Paul and other Bible characters and their discovery of freedom to be themselves. As in Susan's case, they may be ready to receive pastoral care and nurture. Like her they may, with the help of the church and through the work of the Holy Spirit, come to recognize and experience the amazing love of God which gives them an identity and freedom to be themselves, the kind of person God intends them to be. Yes but, when and how does it happen? Does it happen all at once? Does it resolve all our problems? Will it remove inward conflicts and eradicate confusing contradictions?

The answer to all those proper questions must begin with the reminder that God is love and that his love never ceases and never fails (see 1 Corinthians 13). Long before we were aware of it, God loved us. 'God proves his love for us in that while we still were sinners Christ died for us' (Romans 5.8). God has not stopped and will never stop loving us. All too often, however, we live either in ignorance, or have a rather vague notion, of it. But when we recognize that love and respond in gratitude to it; when we express faith in Jesus Christ and begin to follow him, then we experience a renewal of our person in the love of Christ. There is a sense in which the person God intended us to be is restored to us. No, it doesn't happen all at once. The process happens over a long time – over a lifetime for most of us – but knowing that it is happening gives an ultimate meaning, freedom and direction to our life.

Faith in Christ offers us a new primary relationship with the personal source from which all human love and personal relationships, however disfigured, flow. Perhaps it is in this context that we can understand afresh Christ's requirement of our need to be 'born again' (John 3.1–10), to rediscover our 'sonship' and 'daughtership' in Christ, to become a child again and grow up all over again, grounded in the confidence of this new relationship of love. It is in the light of this new love that our inner 'child' is helped to grow into the person we were created to be – our true self.

Am I free to be me?

In the light of Susan's experience, which is shared by many others, and the question she posed, it is difficult to deny the power of inherited influences to determine the shape and direction of our lives for better or for worse. All the past that has gone into making us has got to be faced up to and owned. The luggage in the suitcases, inherited from our family and the network of our relationships, can't be disregarded. But the knowledge and conviction of God's love and the reordering of our lives in relation to him can regenerate all our relationships from within and bring new, positive growth towards our fullness of freedom as persons and children of God.

Renewal in the love of Christ and the creative work of his Spirit sets me free to be me and, however long it takes, free to become the person God wants me to be.

3

God is great – pity about the church

Sitting in a church pew on a regular basis can be a salutary experience. My family have been telling me that for years, of course, and many a Sunday lunch has been punctuated by pertinent and painful comments on the subject. However, now that I have become pew fodder myself, the remarks of the Queen of Sheba, when she had seen the splendour of King Solomon's court, come all too readily to mind – 'the half had not been told me' (2 Chronicles 9.6).

It is common knowledge that many people, including those most committed to it, have a love-hate relationship with the church as an institution. It is capable of producing the contradictory emotions of admiration and anger. And, though I have never engaged in negative criticism of an institution that has nurtured me in discipleship and employed me in leadership, nevertheless I have not been averse to putting proper questions to it, or poking fun at it, when occasion demanded. Such an open stance stood me in good stead when I met with Gill, Joan and Naomi, affectionately nicknamed the Bamford Three.

The Bamford Three

They were three young mothers, each with a lively faith, an enquiring mind and an infectious, if somewhat argumentative, personality. I initially nicknamed them 'the blessed trinity', for their faith and frankness was a godsend. It transformed a rather dull and damp afternoon into an informative, inspiring and at times uncomfortable encounter.

They had volunteered to provide refreshments for a weary band of walkers as we passed through their particular parish. With an eye for the main chance, however, they weren't going to let their bishop off merely with a cup of tea and a bun. They had other things to serve up, some of which were heart-warming, a few were not immediately palatable, but all were presented with a gracious conviction.

The crux of their concern was the contradictions they were having to live with in their desire to be true to God and to be loyal to the church. It wasn't a 'moan' session. To begin with it was more of a praise session. These young women had in recent years come to faith in Christ. There was a touching freshness about their belief in the reality of God. And there was a corresponding realism about the way they expected their faith to be worked out in practice. In no way were they living on a spiritual cloud nine. The first flush of enthusiasm as new Christians had long gone. They were encountering the hard graft of applying Christian values, standards and priorities to their private and public lives and to their network of relationships within the local community. It wasn't easy.

Though they fully understood that the way of Christian discipleship was a difficult one, they were thrilled with their experience of God and the gospel. It was intensely moving to listen to their personal testimonies of what God meant to them and how he had changed their lives. Their vocabulary was wonderfully free from religious jargon. Their references to God, while fairly earthy, were neither cheap nor matey. There was a sense of awe and amazement that God should have taken such an interest in them. Nevertheless, they were struggling with the apparent inconsistencies between their experience of God and some of their experiences of the church. At one point in the conversation Gill actually said, 'Jesus is great', and Naomi, as quick as a flash, added, 'Yes, but it's a pity about the church'. She was embarrassed as soon as she'd said it, but she needn't have been. She was simply echoing the feelings of many and, as we talked, the Bamford Three pinpointed concerns which I have heard again and again in a whole variety of settings and from a wide cross-section of people.

An insatiable appetite

'The church seems at times to be more demanding than God', is the way Joan explained it, and in doing so voiced an anxiety that others share, including me. The busyness of the church and its insatiable appetite for involving people in its activities is often a threat to the proper development of the life of faith.

I recall the time when I was looking for my first job as a young curate. One particular vicar wrote to me and invited me to join his staff team. As an incentive he sent me a copy of the parish magazine and drew my attention to pages eight, nine and ten which contained the monthly diary of the church's activities. 'We are a very busy church,' he told me. It was the understatement of the year. They weren't just busy, they were positively frenetic. They seemed to be bothering God every minute of every day and swallowing up the lives of people in the process.

I didn't go to that particular job. It wasn't that I was scared of hard work, but the demands outlined on pages eight, nine and ten of the parish magazine seemed to me to leave little space for people to develop a life outside that of the local church. The church programme had all the characteristics of a treadmill. Whatever you do, don't stop or the whole system will grind to a halt.

That was the problem being faced by the Bamford Three and many others like them. They had a wonderful network of relationships across their families and across their community in which to share their excitement about God and the gospel, but they were torn with the need to be loyal to the church and its demands upon their time and skills to keep the institution going. Why be excited about God when you can be exhausted by the church?

We might well say that they didn't have to attend everything that the church laid on for them and, of course, they didn't. But that is not always as easy as it sounds. Having been a minister in seven different churches, I confess that it is possible for excessive busy-ness to be geared more towards the enlargement of the minister's ego and the church's status, than the development of the kingdom of God. And sometimes the smaller the congregation the greater the expectation, for those who are willing, to be involved in everything. It can be not only energy-sapping but also soul-destroying.

It isn't always the fault of the ministers. Often they are the victims. Ministers' wives, or husbands for that matter, all have their own horror stories to tell of the excessive demands made upon their partners and their family life by the church, that is, by the people who are members of it. They demand attention and accessibility. They want their minister to be available to them at all times and they don't always make allowances for the fact that he or she may have family responsibilities. Sometimes the demand has the character of emotional blackmail and, to save trouble, the demands are met and unhealthy dependency levels rise as a result.

I recall on one occasion being an embarrassed listener to an animated conversation between a minister and his wife. He was clearly overworking yet he insisted on answering every demand that people made upon him, including a fairly innocuous one that came during a mealtime. He apologized, rose from the table, put on his coat and was about to leave when his wife said, 'Darling, must you go now?' 'Yes, dear,' he replied, 'I really mustn't let them down.' 'Why?' she persisted. 'Why must you be the one to answer every single demand that people make upon you? Does it really all depend on you? After all, there's always God!' She smiled as she said it, but I had a feeling that that was for my benefit. There was something fairly serious and rather unhealthy taking place in that home and family.

The Bamford Three were right. The church, it seemed, was being more demanding than God. Instinctively they knew that freedom in Christ ought not to mean a form of captivity imposed by the institutional church. In any healthy family, including the family of the church, individuals need space in order to grow. God doesn't treat us like children whose every moment must be accounted for and whose every activity must be supervised. He trusts us as adults, allowing us freedom to develop, space to grow and time to nurture relationships in the world as well as in the church.

It's duty that keeps me going

But if a demanding busyness was producing one set of contradictions, a debilitating boredom was responsible for another. It was a topic mentioned not just by the three young mums, it was part of a not-so-hidden agenda that kept coming to the surface on successive stages of my pastoral walks. It was not limited to the young but was a concern expressed by all ages – and by some surprising people. The young, of course, were fairly forthright in their comments, for 'boring' is an expression that they tend to use a lot, to devastating effect. Older folk were more subtle and sophisticated in their vocabulary but it amounted to the same thing in the end. It was summed up by Dorothy, a devout Christian of long standing, who said to me, somewhat nervously, 'I find, these days, that I'm going off church. It's only duty that's keeping me going.'

Now I have no intention of criticizing the concept of duty, quite the reverse, for it has been my salvation on many occasions. Paul's words to the young Timothy, 'Do all the duties of your calling' (2 Timothy 4.5, NEB), have been a source of encouragement to me and millions of others over the years. Circumstances may be threatening to overwhelm us and we don't quite know where to turn, for even God seems distant. Our deliverance, our ability to hold on until the darkness passes and we begin to see the way ahead, comes from doing those things that we are called to do. Those things it is our duty to do. The priest's ministry may be collapsing around him, but the Eucharist will be celebrated, the sick will be visited and the children will be baptized. Politicians may be up to their eyes in controversy, ridiculed by friend and foe alike, but the needs of their constituents will remain paramount and the weekly surgery sacrosanct. The nurse in hospital, the presenter of a radio programme or the mother of young children may all be demoralized and distraught at the prospect of an uncertain future – but the immediate needs of the patient, the listener and the family will be met. Duty will see them through until such time as the way ahead seems clear.

Duty is not a dirty word. I thank God for it. And to Dorothy and others like her my reference to Paul's words to Timothy, and a sharing of my own experience with them, seemed to be of help. There are times when, for all of us, duty keeps us going against the odds until such time as the shadows lift and the sun breaks through. Besides, regular attendance at worship along with our brothers and sisters in Christ is part of our Christian duty (Hebrews 10.25). Nevertheless, to take part in the worship of Almighty God in the presence of the risen Christ should be a delight as well as a duty. Patient endurance should not be the hallmark of our attitude in church. True worship is life-enhancing and life-transforming. Metaphorically speaking we should emerge from it with a spring in our step rather than a ball and chain round our ankle.

Sadly, it is not always so and boring is an all too accurate description. But there are others. It was James, a long-distance lorry driver, who said, 'I find it difficult to relate it to the world I occupy from Monday to Saturday,' and Sandra, his wife, chipped in with, 'It's driving my two teenagers round the bend.' Alex, a quantity surveyor, expressed his feelings thus: 'From the moment I enter church for Sunday morning worship to the moment I leave via the coffee break I am overwhelmed by an avalanche of words. Even some of the hymns are sung over and over as though God wasn't listening the first time.' But it was Brenda's slightly shocking comments that made me roar with laughter while, at the same time, feeling a rather painful embarrassment. A mature and intelligent Christian, she said, 'Last Sunday morning I found what was happening in my local church so irritatingly divorced from the needs, perplexities and contradictions of the world, and my life within it, that I nipped out and did a quick bit of shopping in the local supermarket. There, at least, I seemed to be in touch with reality.'

Begging the question

Brenda's action may be considered extreme but, together with all the other comments mentioned above, it was an indication of the frustration being felt as people struggled with the contradictions of their love for God and their loyalty to the church.

It begs several questions, of course, about motivation. Do we approach worship with a subjectivity that makes its primary objective the meeting of our own personal needs? That is bound to produce frustration and disappointment and it ignores the corporate nature of worship. Do we place the church in the same category as some of our other leisure-time activities – films, theatre, sport, travel, gardening – and disparagingly compare its entertainment value? Sadly, some people do. But such an attitude misses the whole point. While it is rarely possible for us to be totally objective in worship, is not the true motivation for going to church to meet with the living God? This not only requires a singleness of mind on the part of those who come to worship and a creative imagination on the part of those who lead it, but also an openness to God's Spirit on the part of both.

Despite the statistics of decline and the premature obituaries being written about the institutional church I believe that there is a greater commitment among church members today than I have ever known. But far from leading to complacency, that should increase the institutional church's sense of urgency. The research of sociologists like Grace Davie, recorded in her book, *Religion in Britain since 1945*, has revealed evidence of a widespread residual belief in God. It is a fact borne out by the increasing interest in spirituality and, perhaps, by the presence of the 'Spirit Zone' in the Millennium Dome. It is my conviction, therefore, that these are days of real urgency and opportunity for the church. People not only need God; when they come to church it is God they want to meet. They don't want a deep layer of humanism, however sincere and laudable, covered by a thin veneer of religion. They want to meet with the living God. They want a church which relates to them where they are in society and, at the same time, has a prophetic word for that society.

It was David who expressed the vision so helpfully. He was a senior civil servant who had taken the day off to walk with me along a fairly strenuous part of the journey. He was wearing all the proper gear, because walking was his hobby. 'It gives me time to think,' he said, and clearly he'd been thinking a great deal.

'When I go to my local church, bishop, I don't want to be hassled by people who want to use me for their own ends. I don't want to be overlaid with guilt about things I haven't done nor do I wish to be unceasingly exhorted to do better. I want to meet with God. To give him thanks for his continued patience with me and goodness to me. To bring my pressurized and fragmented life and work to him and to ask forgiveness for those occasions when I have failed both him and myself. To seek his help in living the life of faith in today's world and, along with my brothers and sisters in Christ, to put myself at his disposal for service in that world.

'We all know that there is something radically amiss in our society. I want to belong to a church with the insight to see contemporary society as it is, the wisdom to know God's ideal purpose for it, the courage to speak God's word to it, however uncomfortable that may be, and the ability to enable its members to know and to play their part in witnessing effectively and with integrity to that society. It's a tall order I know,' he said, 'but it is worth aiming at and working for, that's why I hang in there despite the discouragement of the church's divisions and, on occasions, its apparent lack of love.'

Whatever happened to love?

I found David's comments immensely hopeful. They affirmed the prophetic role of the church in society. They were realistic about his own need of help from the church and his determination to remain loyal to it. At the same time his comments were honest in pinpointing one of the greatest 'switch-off' points that people have in connection with the church. Busyness and boredom may try the patience of some and, sadly, result in their giving up on the church. But it is bitter and public divisions within the church that cause the greatest concern. They produce the most painful and trying contradiction between people's love for God and their loyalty to the church. They not only cause some to leave the church, they also deter others from joining it.

Thankfully, of course, there are many local churches which are genuine communities of love. The love of God is clearly reflected in and demonstrated by the congregations. It has little to do with large numbers or beautiful liturgy but it has much to do with people paying attention to other people, putting the interests of others before their own, and being motivated by the love of God. However, there are others where divisions are bitter and of long standing. Where love, humility and compassion are conspicuous by their absence and warring factions within the congregation not only make things difficult for the minister but also for God himself (see Matthew 13.58). The classic case was during a church meeting which was discussing the introduction of the Peace, that is, members of the congregation shaking hands with those near to them, during the Eucharist. The discussion was abruptly short-circuited when one rather belligerent gentleman declared, 'If the Peace comes to this church there'll be war!'

As a church leader it was assumed, since I tended to be present only on special occasions when congregations were large and the mood was celebratory, that I always saw the church at its best. That assumption was false. I had enough pastoral experience and spiritual 'nous' to recognize when things were deeply wrong in a church. No amount of ecclesiastical window dressing can hide division either at local or national level. Besides, I have been on the receiving end of too many disputing deputations from local churches to remain naive about the reality of a situation.

And, of course, I was in the firing line when the

Church of England decided to ordain women priests. It was an amazing and, at times, harrowing experience. I had spoken in the famous debate at General Synod for a joyful rather than reluctant acceptance of women in the priesthood. In the weeks that followed, however, I was appalled by the attitudes of some Christian people on both sides of that particular divide.

What was difficult to come to terms with was the contradiction of seeing some of my brothers and sisters in Christ behaving with deplorable discourtesy and verbal venom towards those of their number who disagreed with their point of view. To be firm in our convictions is one thing but to be humiliatingly dismissive of a brother or sister in Christ is, to my mind, unacceptable, ungodly and totally lacking in love. By its very nature the church is a place where strong feelings are held and expressed. That is understandable, for the truths of God and the gospel are very important to us and we are to contend earnestly for them. But the Scriptures are clear. In speaking the truth, as we see it, we are to do so with love as well as conviction (Ephesians 4.15). There were moments during that particular period, and some times since, when I found myself wondering, 'Whatever happened to love?'

Love is alive and well

The more I meet with and listen to ordinary folk and their stories of faith, however, the more convinced I become that love is alive and well and in plentiful supply. The most heart-warming aspect of my pastoral walks was not just the honesty and frankness of those like the Bamford Three, and others like Dorothy, James, Sandra, David and Brenda, it was their continued commitment to God and the church. Their willingness to express their anxiety about certain aspects of the church's life was a measure of their love for it and their concern lest that love should grow cold. There may have been a sense of duty about it. Perhaps their sense of loyalty was stronger than their feelings of disillusionment. But I believe there was much more to it than that.

People are not fools. They know, for every Eucharist reminds them of it, that in Jesus Christ they are linked with their brothers and sisters in every land and in every age as members of the body of Christ, the Church, which Christ loves and for which he died (Ephesians 5.25). They also know that that universal Church, including their own particular local expression of it, is made up of ordinary, sinful, sincere, complex, changeable, often bewildered and perplexed people like themselves. They sometimes find it hard to grasp, but are humbled and excited when they do, that God wishes to use them as partners with him showing his love to the world. They can accept that the contradictions they have to live with are largely the cost of being part of a church which is placed in the midst of a contradictory and somewhat broken world. They sometimes find the contradictions painful but they are ready to live with them as long as the church encourages and enables them to do so by being less concerned with the minutiae and sectional interests of its own institutional life and more committed to helping them to be the church in the world.

Perhaps, instinctively, they endorse the twin description I have heard given of the church as a kindergarten and hospital. In other words its occasional awfulness is the result of being a place where people are literally at their most childish and where people expose their wounds. But, borrowing a phrase from the world of sport, it has also been described as a training ground. A place where, despite its faults and failings, its sins and shortcomings, its weaknesses and frustrations, it provides a constant input of God's love in word and prayer and sacrament. Every day and every week there are reminders of the unmerited love and generous grace of God extended to all who care to receive it.

It is a place of nurture and growth, where we find our real selves by giving ourselves away in love to God and neighbour. It is a place where wounded humanity is welcomed and healing takes place from the inside out. Like the wounds of Christ, the scars are not erased, but transfigured, as we are prepared for our destiny when we shall be like Christ and see him as he is (1 John 3.2).

I believe it is that vision which can help us live with the contradictions we all experience between our love for God and our loyalty to the institution church. Perhaps I can best complete this chapter with a personal testimony to that vision.

A personal testimony

I was nurtured and grew to manhood within the Church of Ireland. At the age of 19 I had an experience of conversion during an evangelistic mission in my own parish church. Some years later I was ordained into the

Church of England and circumstances determined that my first sermon as a new deacon was in the church of my nurture and conversion in Belfast. It is possible, my readers may understand, for those newly ordained to believe, somewhat mistakenly, that they are God's gift to the church. Accordingly, in my arrogance, I was geared up to tell the assembled church congregation, somewhat disparagingly I fear, that despite the fact that I was baptized at that font, confirmed at those chancel steps and received Holy Communion at this table, it wasn't until I was 19 years old that I was converted and came in touch with the real thing!

As I climbed the pulpit steps, however, what I can only describe as an experience of the Spirit took place, and large parts of my sermon had to be discarded. Arrogance was replaced with an amazing awareness of the goodness and grace of God allied to the revelation that it wasn't in spite of baptism, confirmation and Holy Communion that I had been converted and later ordained. Rather it was because of them that my conversion and ordination took place. While I was still too preoccupied, too selfish or too thick to understand, God, through his institutional church, held on to me until the penny dropped. He patiently watched over me and through word and sacrament, and the commitment of Sunday school teachers and the leaders of various youth organizations, prepared me for what lay ahead.

That's why I believe that God is great and the gospel is wonderful. It is also why, despite its shortcomings, I love the church. It persevered with me despite my shortcomings – and still does!

4

Jesus is Lord – but not always

After a solid day's walking along the hard pavements of one of south London's vast urban areas it was just what the doctor ordered – a foretaste of heaven, a microcosm of the kingdom of God. 'It' was a multicultural evening held in an inner-city church centre that was packed to the rafters. The rich and exciting aroma of Afro-Caribbean food permeated the whole atmosphere. The enthusiastic hubbub of people talking in a dozen different languages and dialects was reminiscent of the Day of Pentecost. Rich and poor, black and white, young and old, male and female, combined to create a wonderfully inclusive gathering.

But Colette wasn't there. She was at home with her husband Carl and their two young children.

A divided heart?

Two years earlier I had baptized the two children and confirmed Colette at a great initiation service in the cathedral. Carl was there to encourage and support them but, when asked about his own priorities for life, was adamant that he wasn't interested in entering beyond the fringe of the church. It was an attitude he still maintained two years on and it was part of the story Colette had shared with me as we walked the streets of London that afternoon.

She and Carl, both of Nigerian origin, were very much in love. Colette was a sister midwife, Carl was a solicitor. They agreed to differ on religion. She was a devout Christian. He was an agnostic. It was a familiar story and one I have encountered often across the country and across the church as couples have struggled with the challenging, sometimes painful, contradiction of Christian allegiance within the home. 'Who's in charge?' may seem like a strange question in the circumstances but, as Carl and Colette agreed, it helped to focus the dilemma they often faced.

I recall a motto, popular when I was a newly-wed and displayed prominently in many Christian homes at the time. It read, 'Christ is the Head of this household, the unseen guest at every meal, the silent listener to every conversation.' I have seen the motto hanging in some homes where the occupants seemed to be in a permanent state of verbal warfare. For different reasons, it would have been inappropriate in the home of Carl and Colette. They were only too well aware of the contradictions that occasionally arose as a result of the latter's devotion to Christ and the former's agnostic stance. Nevertheless, the motto does serve to pose the question: just what did it mean in that home and family for Colette to say and believe that 'Jesus is Lord'?

It wasn't just a slogan. As far as she was concerned it was a way of life. Its implications had to be worked out in the way the children were brought up, in the priorities that were set for home and family, and in her relationship with Carl. It also had ramifications for the world of work, for family friendships and for the vexed question of finance, including the practice of tithing. Fortunately, when it came to decision-making and priority-setting, Colette had enough common sense to realize that it was neither right, nor particularly Christian, to say, 'Jesus is Lord, whatever he says goes, and that's the end of the matter.' Though she was aware that the Bible had certain things to say on the subject, she knew there were no detailed blueprints for many aspects of her domestic life, especially when one partner in the relationship was an agnostic. Besides, Carl's agnostic attitude was held with integrity and could not be gazumped by an appeal to 'Jesus as Lord' and the so-called end of the matter.

There were times when what Colette perceived as the legitimate claims of Christ conflicted sharply with the sincerely held views of Carl. Just how much money, for instance, should be given from the family budget for the work of the church? And what about the baptism of the children? Would Carl be happy to listen to godparents taking vows for his children's spiritual welfare which he couldn't with integrity endorse? And would Colette be frustrated in her desire to follow Jesus by her marital responsibilities towards Carl?

It wasn't always easy. Sometimes the demands of the local church were insensitive and Carl felt left out. At other times he allowed his agnosticism to become a little barbed and dismissive of Colette's faith. On occasions there was anger expressed, jealousy experienced and periodically there were tears shed. Sometimes humour relieved the tension, like the night when Carl heard a rather crass church leader say to Colette, 'We're praying flat out for your husband to be converted.' Carl saw the funny side and said to his wife, 'This lot are out to get me. Take me home quick before they hang my scalp on their totem pole.'

But as so often happens in these situations, love and common sense found a way to live with the contradictions. Neither Carl nor Colette believed that compromise was a dirty word. They didn't see it as another name for second best. It didn't mean a 'some you win and some you lose' kind of scenario. Rather, with a determination to keep the lines of communication, understanding and respect fully open between them, they turned the win/lose scenario into a win/win situation. Colette believed that since all love came from God, he was responsible for the love between herself and Carl. Carl had some doubts about the concept of God but none whatsoever about the quality of the love they shared. It proved to be a solid base on which to live with and grow through contradiction. Carl recognized that Colette was a more whole person as a result of her faith, and encouraged her in it. Colette was convinced of the sincerity of Carl's agnostic view and respected him for it. She acknowledged Jesus as Lord and, when occasion demanded, put the welfare of her relationship with her husband and family first.

That's why she wasn't at the multicultural evening

in the church centre. She missed out on a glorious event which, ironically, ended with the tumultuous singing of the hymn 'Jesus is Lord'. Carl had been away on a week's conference and had just returned that evening. Colette felt it right to pass up on the party and the singing of the glory songs in order to be with her husband at home. She knew that love and holiness doesn't flourish by neglecting family responsibilities. I had the feeling that she'd made the right choice and one that not only affirmed her belief that 'Jesus is Lord' but also quietly answered the question, 'Who's in charge?'

Ambition

With Jonathan, however, it wasn't quite so easy to discover who was in charge. Someone had told him that he was clearly destined for higher things. Not only did he believe them, he also seemed hell-bent on proving them right. And, strangely, he had no hesitation in telling me about it. So, as we walked along the right of way across a beautiful part of the Yorkshire dales, I tried to get a gentle message across to him by telling him of my experience in the House of Lords.

In that House of many archaic conventions there is one rather touching one in connection with maiden speeches. When a noble lord or lady makes a maiden speech it is the custom not to be politically controversial. This enables those speakers who follow after in the debate to observe the convention of offering congratulations, often in fulsome terms, to the noble lord or baroness in question.

My maiden speech, during a debate on cuts in higher education budgets, sailed fairly close to the controversial wind. Nevertheless, one noble lord after another, and there were 40 speeches following mine, graciously observed the convention. The maiden speech of the Right Reverend Prelate was described in glowing terms and he was warmly congratulated for it. Words like, 'The eloquence and passion of the Right Reverend Prelate have been a source of inspiration to this House today and we look forward to many similar contributions in the future', flowed from the lips of earls, viscounts and baronesses. It was all very gratifying, embarrassing, and dangerous. Dangerous, that is, if you actually took the comments seriously and began to believe that you were the church's equivalent to Lloyd George or Winston Churchill! Reality was restored, however, at one's next speech when the convention didn't apply and, metaphorically speaking, the gloves were off and it was open season on bishops.

Jonathan smiled at my story but didn't quite get the message. He seemed more concerned to discover how long bishops had to wait before they got into the House of Lords and I had the feeling, almost, that he was wanting to put a provisional date in his diary. He had been ordained some 12 years before and was a popular vicar of a large parish. He was running his congregation ragged with his activism, being the kind of person who had ten new ideas before breakfast each day and had them implemented before lunch. One of his flock who was with me on the walk said, in a moment of indiscretion and with a naughty twinkle in her eye,

'Our vicar hopes to be a bishop one day.' I made a mental note to pray that he might be delivered from such a fate. Seriously though, as I talked with him it became obvious that he was a driven person. He was perpetually in pursuit of an ambition to make it big in the church. He no doubt believed that 'Jesus is Lord' but he clearly lived and worked as though Jonathan was very much in control and with energetic application would produce the goods.

He was not alone. Some clergy are past masters at playing the humility game while surreptitiously pushing their own claims for promotion or, as it is called in the church, preferment. One classic case was the priest who had spent most of his life in chaplaincy work and was wanting to come into what he called 'mainstream' ministry. I assumed that he meant he wanted to become the vicar of a parish and asked him what kind of thing he had in mind. He replied, 'I think I would slot in most easily at the suffragan bishop level.' I was astonished at his reply but at least he was honest. Ambition was the name of the game. And why not?

What's wrong with it?

Is ambition a bad thing? Was Jonathan, and are others like him, wrong to have ambitions for so-called major jobs in society or in the church? Why is ambition considered something to be commended and applauded in the secular world of business, education and science, for instance, and thought to be rather suspect in the church? It is an important question, for all too easily we can misunderstand the motives of others and unfairly criticize them.

I believe that there is a proper place for ambition in all walks of life and certainly in the Christian life. As we grow older and more experienced in our profession it is both natural and right to want to be engaged in what has been called 'the ordering of the world and ourselves' and to wish to do it more widely, on a larger canvas and on a bigger stage. Not everyone wants to do this but those who do ought not to be considered suspect or less spiritual than others. It is part of our responsibility as human beings, as well as part of stewardship as Christians, not only to use our God-given abilities to their fullest capacity but also to encourage and enable others to do the same.

To my mind there is no real conflict between our call to be servants of God and our desire to paint, as it were, on a larger canvas. If the latter enables us to make choices, set priorities, and be stretched intellectually and spiritually, so that we are better equipped to serve others, it ought to be encouraged rather than despised. However, there is all the difference in the world between selfish ambition and ambition for gospel and kingdom priorities. It was clearly the former that Shakespeare had in mind when he wrote:

> Cromwell, I charge thee, fling away ambition:
> By that sin fell the angels; how can man then,
> The image of his Maker, hope to win by 't?
>
> (Henry VIII III.2)

It was in seeking to usurp the place of God that the angels fell. Those who proclaim Jesus is Lord and then, to all intents and purposes, dispense with his services and take on the role themselves are, likewise, living dangerously. Ambition which manipulates or diminishes others, which pushes them to one side or tramples on them in order to get to the top, is not godly ambition. Sadly, often in society and from time to time in the church, there are those who, in seeking to create a name for themselves, have engaged in the character assassination of others. Such selfish and ambitious behaviour by Christians, either in society or in the church, is a denial of the Lordship of Christ. 'Jesus is Lord', but, in their case, not always.

However, ambition which promotes gospel and kingdom priorities and which pursues wider responsibility in order to serve others better is of a different calibre. It doesn't walk over others. It is stamped with humility. Indeed, it bears the character of childlikeness and Christlikeness:

> An argument arose among them as to which one of them was the greatest. But, Jesus, aware of their inner thoughts, took a little child and put it by his side, and said to them, 'Whoever welcomes this child in my name welcomes me, and whoever welcomes me welcomes the one who sent me; for the least among all of you is the greatest.'
>
> (Luke 9.46–48)

> 'For who is greater', [said Jesus] 'the one who is at table or the one who serves? Is it not the one at the table? But I am among you as one who serves.'
>
> (Luke 22.27)

The humility of the servant need not be in conflict with vibrant ambition, as long as that ambition reflects rather than replaces the Lordship of Christ.

The call of God

Geoffrey's ambition was certainly vibrant but its source was questionable. He was twisted and bitter and lost no time in having a go at his bishop. He talked almost as fast as he walked, so it was a fairly exhausting mile and a half in more senses than one. A teacher by profession, he was upset that the Church refused to endorse what he considered to be an incontrovertible call from God to be ordained. He was in no mood to hear weasel words. God had called him; indeed, he even went as far as to claim that God had told him to be ordained. What right, therefore, had the Church to turn him down? Because of his perceived rejection Geoffrey had stopped going to his local church. The iron had entered into his soul. It was one of the saddest moments of my journey. What possible response can you make to the claim, 'God has told me'? Besides, at that particular moment, Geoffrey was not in any mood to listen to scriptural teaching let alone human reason. He just wasn't thinking biblically or logically. He had no doubt whatsoever that Jesus is Lord – but not, apparently, of the Church and its discernment about his call to be ordained.

Martha's attitude was in complete contrast. She didn't claim divine warrant for anything. She certainly didn't want to be ordained. God forbid! She just got on with her life of love and service without fuss and without any desire for reward or recognition. The thought that she might have been specially called by God to do what she did in the local church and community had never entered her head. She would have been embarrassed by the mere suggestion. Yet the common testimony of those who knew her was that she was a modern-day saint whose goodness and service to others was free of self-interest.

I must confess the road ahead seemed easier when walking alongside Martha. But the comparison with Geoffrey did raise interesting questions in my mind and in my memory regarding the concept of the call of God. Is it always clear cut? Is it always necessary? Does the belief that Jesus is Lord mean that we must not do anything, especially anything of significance, unless he gives us the all-clear? Do we expect him, as it were, to have a finger in every pie? Will we be guilty of disobedience if we go it alone?

Speaking from personal experience there have been times when, though I didn't dare make the kind of assertion that Geoffrey did, I was convinced that God was wanting me to do certain things. As a young Christian it seemed that God gave me either so-called 'signs' or very strong circumstantial evidence to follow a certain course of action. This is not unusual and there is scriptural precedent for that kind of guidance being particularly important in the early days of our journey of faith.

A plastic duck

However, as the years progressed, there was a subtle change in this matter of discerning the call of God. It came about not so much by my lack of faith, at least I hope not, but by the sheer complexity of the circumstances facing me, including the natural complexity of my own personality. There were times when, having been invited to do a specific piece of work, it was hard to separate false modesty from foolish pride. On other occasions it was not always easy to discover whether I was being called by God, manipulated by men, or dragged by circumstances towards some particular decision.

Like many others in such situations, where the magnitude of the task being presented was equalled only by the gigantic sense of personal inadequacy being experienced, I had to leave it to the Church, through its chosen representatives, to discern the call of God for me. If the Church was asking me to become a bishop, for instance, then because I believed that Jesus is Lord of the Church I had to have a very good reason for saying no to its invitation. Often decisions had to be taken by the application of one's own mind on the basis of the information available – and accompanied by a great deal of prayer and not a little faith.

Frequently the confirmation that the decision was the right one only came afterwards. Sometimes the storm that engulfed me in the wake of the decision caused me, momentarily, to question its validity. Indeed, as I have progressed through my life and work it has sometimes felt, to quote some words from the autobiography of Frank Muir, *A Kentish Lad*, 'that I had as much control over my progress as a plastic duck in a jacuzzi'. There were moments when my heart said, 'Jesus is Lord' and my head, conscious of the circumstances surrounding me, was saying, 'but not always'.

However, since life is lived looking forwards and understood looking backwards, it has always been possible to trace the good purposes of God in retrospect. Despite appearances and feelings to the contrary Jesus had been exercising his Lordship in a whole variety of ways. I discovered that he is Lord in the storm as well as Lord in the calm. He is Lord in failure as well as Lord in success. He is Lord in sickness as well as Lord in health.

'Jesus Christ is Lord' is probably the earliest Christian creed. The classic Bible passage containing it is found in St Paul's letter to the Philippians (2.6–11), where he describes the action of God in response to the staggering humility of Jesus, in birth, life and death. His response was one of exaltation. Having raised Jesus from death he also raised him to glory and gave him 'the name that is above every name' and placed him in a position of universal authority.

Such action on the part of God requires those of us who believe that 'Jesus Christ is Lord' to commit ourselves to make good that confession in every area of our own lives as well as that of society. But such an action by God in the face of the cross which, by any human standards, was an ignominious disaster, also gives us confidence to live our lives with joyful freedom in Christ. Not, as it were, always looking over our shoulders to see if he's giving us the thumbs up before we do anything. God desires us to grow towards maturity and completeness in Christ (Ephesians 4.13–15), but growth requires space and God, in his wisdom, gives us that space. He allows us the freedom to think, make choices, make mistakes, suffer failure or achieve success – and live with the contradictions that such complexity produces.

Throughout it all, however, in bad times as well as good, JESUS CHRIST IS LORD.

5

Believing with your fingers crossed

People don't always believe or behave in the way preachers imagine they should.

It was a lesson I learnt early in life. As a young vicar I had preached my heart out at a special service one Sunday evening. The church was crowded and for 25 minutes I thundered on the doctrine of justification by faith. I felt that the sermon had been accessible to the congregation and free from religious jargon. 'We find acceptance with God not on the basis of what we have done but by trusting in what Jesus Christ has done for us on the cross. Faith rather than works is required.' As far as I was concerned the message was loud and clear.

But not to Ron. He bounced up to me enthusiastically afterwards to congratulate me on my sermon. 'That was really great, vicar, very encouraging. You're absolutely right, and it's something I've always believed, we must try our hardest, do our best, and God will see us all right in the end.'

I didn't know whether to laugh or cry. In the event I

did neither. Instead, I vowed never to be overconfident in my ability as a teacher or preacher. I also made a mental note always to ask myself a question after I had preached, namely, 'How do I know what I have said until I know what you have heard?' The fact that 300 people in the pews appear to be hanging on your every word may be encouraging, but it is no guarantee that they are all hearing the same thing in the same way. And while we must not limit the power of the Holy Spirit to interpret and apply God's word to us, experience leads me to the conviction that people, listening to the same words, often come to different conclusions and form different priorities.

Yorkshire grit

This conviction was certainly borne out on one of my rural walks in the Yorkshire dales. Yorkshire people are known for their bluntness which, in my book, is much to be preferred than blandness. They are also persistent. If they have a concern, they say so and keep saying it. Indeed, like Yorkshire terriers, they only let go in order to get a better grip.

Jack, a local farmer, had such a concern and told me bluntly about it. 'Bishop, I don't believe every part of the Creed. That worries the missus but it doesn't bother me. It's just that when I come to that bit about the Virgin Birth, I can't quite swallow it.' And, with a wickedly humorous look in his eye, he went on, 'I say it, of course – but I keep my fingers crossed when I do.'

Jack's commitment to his local church was impressive.

He was generous, caring and, as far as his ceaselessly busy life would allow, active in the church's work. But he lived with this contradiction which, though he said it didn't bother him, was clearly a concern, or he wouldn't have mentioned it. It was honesty that caused him to do so, and afterwards he acknowledged that he felt better off for having got it off his chest. Apparently he had never felt able to discuss it with anyone other than his wife.

In the brief time we had together I assured him that he was not the first person to have doubts about the Virgin Birth, and although I didn't share his doubts, there were some in the church, and many in society, who did. Nevertheless, the universal Church had held to this tradition for centuries, and for good reason. I didn't criticize him for holding his particular opinion about the Virgin Birth. It seemed more helpful to remind him that the Creed begins with the words 'We believe', indicating that it is a corporate expression of faith. Some, like him, find themselves caught in the tension between the Church's Creed and their own personal beliefs. Many, indeed, have found their personal belief moving from the traditional to more radical and back again to the traditional. The Church is the ideal place to work out our faith. It doesn't condemn us for our personal beliefs but it reminds us of the importance of relating those beliefs to a historic expression of faith which is much more than personal opinion. While respecting Jack's convictions, I suggested he looked again at the matter with the help of his local minister. It might help to resolve his contradiction and, perhaps, give his fingers a rest.

Jack was not unique. While not everyone would share his particular concern, there are many within the church who live with contradictions about the faith and the manner in which they believe and behave. Preachers tend to present their material in reasonably compact packages. The traditional sermon has an introduction, three points, and a conclusion. If the preacher has done their homework the truth they are proclaiming will come across as neat and tidy and convincing. And, in his or her mind, it may be. But out there, in the minds and in the lives of their people, the matter may not be so clear-cut or obvious. There will be fuzzy edges, competing priorities and, perhaps, a contrary experience. These things may not cause the listener to deny what he or she has heard, but often they result in an adjustment being made to bring what has been heard into line with what people are actually experiencing.

There are other ways

Take Margaret, for instance. Unlike Jack, who lived in the same dale, her problem wasn't doctrinal but practical. Her new minister was as keen as mustard. He had recently moved from an inner-city parish and evangelism was very high on his agenda. This became obvious when virtually every sermon he preached, whatever passage of the Bible he started from, ended up with an impassioned exhortation to his congregation to 'go and tell' the gospel story to their neighbours.

Evangelism was also high on Margaret's agenda, in fact she was rather good at it, but if she didn't quite ignore her minister's plea, she radically adjusted it to her own experience of living in the dale. She wasn't quite as blunt as Jack but, being a Yorkshire lass, she made her views clear. 'Bishop Roy, I'm very fond of our new minister, despite the fact that he comes from Lancashire. He'll be all right, when he settles down. He just needs to relax a little bit more. I agree with him about the importance of evangelism but he's muddle-headed in the way he's going about it. So in public and in theory I support him but in private and in practice I do my own thing. I don't want to be disloyal but it's a contradiction I must live with for the moment until the situation becomes a little clearer.'

In certain circumstances I might have gently chided Margaret for her rather patronizing attitude, but I knew the position too well for that. She had lived in the dale for 40 years and knew everyone else who lived there, indeed, they mostly knew each other. The scenic environment was truly magnificent but daily life was tough and demanding for those, like Margaret, who farmed in the dale. They were aware of each other's joys and sorrows, they helped each other at times of disaster, for instance when snow, wind and rain came at lambing time and threatened their flocks and livelihood.

Margaret was a leading figure in the community and, along with others from the church, would visit the sick, keep an eye on the bereaved and run special events for children and young people. She was known and respected for her practical Christianity. She had been sharing the gospel with her neighbours for nigh on 40 years. She instinctively, perhaps, had heeded the words attributed to St Francis of Assisi, 'Preach the gospel everywhere, use words if you must.' For her and others suddenly to become aggressively evangelistic within the relatively small and fairly close-knit dales community would have been pastorally unwise and almost certainly counter-productive.

There was no gap between what she believed and how she behaved, but a little adjustment had to be made between what she was being asked to do and the way she did it. It was a contradiction she could happily live with for the sake of the gospel and, perhaps, until her minister's head cleared!

Head and heart

Brenda's head was anything but clear. As for her heart, she felt it was breaking. I knew she had a serious problem when, as the day's walk began, she asked if I would come and see her after the walk was over. It clearly wasn't a matter we could discuss as we walked in the company of others.

Brenda had been living, somewhat tremulously, with a major contradiction within herself and her family which was made worse by the fact that she couldn't share it with her friends at the church. She recounted her story quietly and with dignity. Her son, Daniel, who was in his early twenties, had told her some months ago that he was gay. To say that she was shocked would be a massive understatement. All her built-in fears and prejudices, and her faint awareness of the church's traditional teaching, rose to the surface as she silently prayed, 'O God, please don't let this be true. Anything but this.' But, as the silent arrow prayer was offered, out went her arms to embrace her son. She didn't know how she was going to cope with the situation, but he was her son, she loved him and, even if she was fearful for his future, she would not reject him.

The weeks that followed were traumatic. A whole cacophony of emotions threatened to destroy the harmony of her life and faith. Shame, guilt, anger and abhorrence vied with one another for prior place in her feelings. Her strong evangelical upbringing and faith was thrown into disarray as she wrestled with the issue, and felt sorry for herself. Slowly, however, her motherly instincts and her Christian love began to replace self-pity. If she felt bewildered and betrayed, what must her son have been going through as he struggled with his sexuality without the support and understanding of his parents and family? His turmoil and isolation must have been terrible to bear. She felt sad and rather ashamed that she had been unaware or, perhaps, insensitive to it.

Her love and faith was presented with another hurdle when Daniel introduced his partner to her. By this time, of course, her husband and her other son and daughters had been let into the secret. Like her, they were shocked but not dismissive. They found it hard to get their minds around it. That this should be happening in their family was unthinkable, but they had to admit that Daniel seemed happier and more fulfilled than they had ever known him. They were gracious, if a little hesitant, in their welcome of Daniel's partner.

But while all this was happening Brenda was having

to cope with the massive contradiction between faith and experience. Her head and her heart were at odds. Her faith screamed loudly that Daniel's lifestyle was wrong. Her experience and love was telling her something different, and she struggled somewhere between the two. It wasn't really helped by the attitude of some within the local church. Daniel still worshipped there when he came to visit his parents but instinctively Brenda knew she couldn't, as yet, share her dilemma with the church family. Instead she had to listen to so many hurtful, ignorant and inaccurate comments about homosexuals, as individuals in the church reacted negatively to sensational media reports on the issue. Sodomites and sinners, perverts, poofs and child-molesters, was how she heard them described.

Brenda was distraught. Though unaware of it, they were talking about her son. They were talking about a fellow-disciple of Christ, one who had been baptized, confirmed and who still worshipped regularly in their church. Though very distressed, and with her deep-seated contradiction still unresolved, such comments made her all the more determined to offer love and support to Daniel and his partner.

I was glad to offer my own friendship and understanding. I believe the gospel required me to do so, as did the House of Bishops' report, *Issues in Human Sexuality*, issued in 1991. While not condoning situations like Daniel's, it is with reference to such that paragraph 5.2 clearly declares:

We stand alongside them in the fellowship of the

> Church, all alike dependent upon the undeserved grace of God. All those who seek to live their lives in Christ owe one another friendship and understanding. It is therefore important that in every congregation such homophiles should find fellow-Christians who will sensitively and naturally provide this for them. Indeed, if it is not done, any profession on the part of the Church that it is committed to openness and learning about the homophile situation can be no more than empty words.

Brenda had not been aware of the bishops' statement and, while she came to recognize that it did not and would not commend Daniel's current lifestyle, she was immensely encouraged and relieved by its compassionate and understanding tone. She wondered why it had never been discussed in her local church. It seemed that there was no room for this kind of openness and learning within that community of faith.

Openness and learning

It is, I believe, this lack of openness that helps to create so many unhelpful contradictions in the life and faith of Christians. The contention of this little book is that contradictions can become the raw material for growth towards maturity in Christ. But there are some contradictions which people endure, particularly in the realm of belief and behaviour, which could be resolved, or made easier to live with, if only there was greater openness and honesty within their local church.

Some of the stories I heard during my walk bore this out and John's was a classic. He hadn't been going to his local church long but was keen to get involved, especially since his enforced early retirement. Naturally I asked him how things were going, and though my question was directed at his life in general it was answered with regard to his life in the church. He frowned slightly and said, 'Bishop, I'm puzzled. Everyone else in my church seems to be a better Christian than I am. They rarely ask questions, whereas I'm full of them. They're always nice, whereas I have my stroppy moments. They don't appear to have problems with the faith whereas I struggle. And God always seems to answer their prayers – or so they keep telling me.

'During a study group last week I said that God didn't always answer my prayers and, anyway, I found it difficult to believe in miracles. I'm afraid it rocked the boat because the hitherto fairly bland atmosphere became a bit rough. Clearly they were not used to people expressing their doubts. At the end of the group session a member of the church's counselling team said he'd love to come and have a chat with me. Though, to be honest, I don't think it's counselling I need, I just want to raise a few of my queries about the faith and get a few answers. I don't find faith easy and I want to know why it appears to be so easy for them. They all seem to believe the same thing in the same way. No one seems to have any doubts about anything. And I'm puzzled because my experience of life is not like that.'

My sympathies were with John. I recall, as a young man newly committed to the faith, not only following the example of older Christians but also adopting their attitudes and using their style of language. It seemed the proper thing to do at the time. But when the time came for me to begin to articulate my faith to others I became uncomfortable with what I was saying. It wasn't that I lacked courage. Rather, I lacked conviction that what I was saying was actually true in my own experience. I was simply saying what I felt my fellow Christians were expecting me to say. But it was often at odds with reality. There was more of the parrot than the prophet about it.

It was a contradiction I couldn't live with and I made a bid for freedom. I'm sure my youthful arrogance was painful to many, and for that I ask their forgiveness, but if I was staking my life on faith in Christ I wanted to be sure it was real rather than sanitized faith. So I began to argue myself clear about the faith, asking questions, raising doubts, challenging attitudes, and coming back to the Bible again and again to check things out. It was helpful to know that Paul was prepared to argue with Peter and that people like Job and the Psalmist were prepared to argue with God and express their doubts and misgivings when necessary.

A happy accident?

I was also helped by a slightly humorous accident, yes accident, that happened to a man who was converted during the same evangelistic mission as I was. He worked in the Belfast shipyards and a few days after his conversion was leaving work, with thousands of others, at the end of the day. He was riding a bicycle at the time and hoped to get away quickly in order to get to the evening mission at the church. But a car, trying to beat the rush, clipped his rear wheel and tumbled him off the bike, bruising his knee, wounding his pride but causing no damage whatsoever to his tongue. Rising from the ground he let loose a string of rich and fruity expletives that would have made the traditional sergeant major blush.

Later that evening he turned up in church looking depressed and feeling disappointed. After the service he made a beeline for the missioner, Canon Keith de Berry, of blessed memory, and told him in no uncertain terms that this Christianity lark didn't work. 'I was told that if anyone was in Christ, he was a new creature, the old was passed away and everything was new [2 Corinthians 5.17]. Well it's not true. Before I became a Christian I swore like a trooper but when I got converted I stopped. I haven't sworn for four days until tonight, when I made up for lost time. The old hasn't passed away at all, and everything is not new.'

The missioner was very wise. 'Tell me,' he said, 'if you had been knocked off your bike a month ago and had sworn as vehemently as you did this evening, would you have been worried about it?' 'Not in the least,' the man replied. 'Well then, don't you think something real has happened to you since you turned to Christ, something that has changed your whole attitude to your old way of life, including swearing?'

Those wise and godly words became a source of great encouragement not only to the man in question but also to me. The fact that there was an element of doubt and struggle and growth within the Christian life marked the authenticity rather than the absence of faith. We are made new in Christ but it doesn't always feel like it and it doesn't happen all at once. We must expect problems, doubts and difficulties as well as joy, peace and fulfilment in the Christian life. It is all part of growing into Christ (Ephesians 4.15) and growing always carries an element of pain and struggle.

It is more open and honest for the church community to reflect the reality of this diverse experience rather than pretend it doesn't exist. The church, after all, is a home for sinners and a school for saints – in that order! The community of faith is meant to be a community of character where the various facets of real life are reflected and where people of faith don't have their diverse and wounded personalities erased but healed and transformed into the likeness of Christ (2 Corinthians 3.18).

A rich diversity

To be honest, it took me a while to come to terms with any suggestion of a diversity of faith and practice within the local church community and I can understand why some find it threatening. As a young vicar I felt threatened by the prospect of division within my congregation. When conflict regarding belief or behaviour arose I was quick to dampen it down with a blanket of blandness. Leaders within the church tended to be chosen for their inability or unwillingness to rock the boat. Unity for the sake of the gospel and the world was the bottom line.

But I believe that my desire for unity was misplaced. On reflection, perhaps, I was looking for the unity of the graveyard where there are no discordant or strident voices of opposition. I think I was more concerned with preserving a united front than presenting both the local church and the local community with a truly biblical view of unity. I saw diversity as a threat to unity whereas unity only becomes meaningful and authentic when it springs from diversity. Both unity and diversity come from God. His grace creates the unity by making us members of the one Body, of which Christ is the Head. It is that same grace, however, given as a gift, that enables every single member of Christ's Body, with their different cultures, temperaments and personalities, to make some significant contribution to the common good (Ephesians 4.7). Together, unity and diversity are an exciting combination.

The unity of the Church, including the local expression of it, is to reflect the character of God, a diversity of persons in a relationship of love. I don't believe that God created such a wealth of diversity within his Church and his world in order to reduce it to a common mould of predictability and boredom. I believe it is the flourishing of diversity; the knitting together, the affirming, the resourcing and equipping of the great wealth of diversity within the body of Christ, that will influence society and promote the mission of God in the world.

I am certainly not advocating the kind of diversity of

faith and practice where anything goes. God forbid. That is chaos not unity. A unity which is based on the character of God must have truth as its hallmark and touchstone. It is when we can argue with one another, disagree with one another, challenge one another's belief and behaviour, on the basis of revealed biblical truth and in the security of a communion of love, that we will have something of vital importance to say to a society torn by division and demanding a moral lead.

6

Brass heavens

I hadn't heard the expression since I was a boy in the back streets of Belfast. And now here it was again on the lips of George as we walked through the heather on a windswept Yorkshire moor. 'The heavens were like brass', he said, and in doing so introduced a topic that was raised again and again during my pastoral walks, namely, unanswered prayer. Those who raised it tended to do so tentatively because personal prayer is considered by many to be a private matter and as for unanswered prayer, that is a problematic and painful contradiction for most of us.

It certainly was for George, a respected lay leader in his local church. Despite his energy, skill and prayers, his small family business had folded two years before. His Christian principles had ensured that his outstanding debts were fully paid but it meant moving into a more moderate house with a consequent change of lifestyle. He didn't blame God for the collapse of his business. Instead, metaphorically speaking, he rolled up his sleeves and began to search for a new job, not an easy task for a 55-year-old. It was then that his faith was thrown into turmoil, though only those close to him knew it, for, despite energetic efforts and constant prayer, he remained unemployed for a further two years. Like others in similar circumstances there was a consequent loss of dignity and self-worth as one job application after another was rejected.

On the morning we walked together across the moor, however, there was a new spring in his step for he had obtained a job the day before. It was not an exciting job nor, indeed, one with prospects. It would not make the best use of his experience and skill, but it was a job and he was grateful for it and said to me, with a slight break in his voice, 'Bishop, it has been a dreadful two years and, despite my prayers, the heavens have been like brass.' It was his rather quaint way of describing the contradiction he had been living with for two long years. He believed in a living God who encouraged the prayers of his children and yet his own prayers, and those of his family at their time of greatest need, had remained unanswered.

A common experience

It was a privilege for me to be allowed to share in George's story, but it was also painful. I didn't have slick answers or trite soundbites to offer. Besides, since God appeared to have kept silent for two years, who was I to rush into the breach with words of dubious wisdom? However, I knew where George had got his 'heavens were like brass' quotation from and this, at least, gave me a starting point to empathize with him. Occurring as it does in Deuteronomy 28.23, he had used it somewhat out of context but, nevertheless, it was an apt description of an experience which very many of us share from time to time. We don't, as it were, seem to be able to get through to God or he to us. The heavens are impenetrable. Our prayers are unanswered and our plight unrelieved. Such silence on the part of God is often hard to bear and frequently impossible to explain.

But it seems that it was ever thus. It is difficult to read certain parts of the Old Testament, for instance, without being forced to the conclusion that God doesn't always answer the prayers of his people. Job, in the midst of his anguish, cried out for God to answer his requests for action and his demands for justice but, in the short term, all he got were the unsought and unconvincing contributions from his so-called comforters. As for the Psalmist he, in a whole variety of circumstances, lamented the fact that God was short on answers to the plight and prayers of his people. In the psalms of lament (Psalms 44; 74; 78; 79; 83; 89, for instance) the great question being asked of God is, How long? How long must we wait for your answer and your action?

In Psalm 44 the writer puts the matter fairly bluntly in the face of the experience of national rejection and disgrace, and asks some unpalatable questions. Can it be that God has fallen asleep and so is unaware of their situation? Has he turned his back on them? The writer's dilemma produces the following outburst:

Rouse yourself! Why do you sleep, O Lord?
Awake, do not cast us off for ever!
Why do you hide your face?
Why do you forget our affliction and oppression?
For we sink down to the dust;
our bodies cling to the ground.
Rise up, and come to our help.
Redeem us for the sake of your steadfast love.

(Psalm 44.23–26)

There is no answer to these questions of the Psalmist. All the people of God can do is to call upon him to help as a sign of his love and devotion. God's failure to act or answer in the way we expect remains a mystery both for individuals and for whole groups of people.

There is, I am sure, some truth in the claim that God always answers our prayers and does so in one of three ways, namely, yes, no, or wait. That is, he grants or refuses our request or, perhaps, he puts it on hold. I dare say that most of us might have experienced each of these answers during our lifetime. However, when we have been going through wilderness experiences like George, it hasn't always been possible to differentiate between a no and a wait. If I had walked with George a week earlier before he got his new job I think he would have said that both answers were equally disappointing if not disastrous. But though his disappointment had been real and his faith had been shaken, he was convinced of the love of God for him. On that basis he had continued to say his prayers and look to God for help during the whole of that dreadful period. 'What else could I do?' he said.

What's the secret?

George's question was rhetorical. Rosemary's was not. She wanted answers not just from God but from me. And, as people often do, she covered her own embarrassment by asking her question in a slightly provocative manner. 'Now then, Bishop, you're the expert on prayer; tell me, what's the secret of successful praying? How do we get answers out of God?'

My reply was, perhaps, predictable but sincere none the less. 'I am not an expert on prayer and may God help and forgive me if I have ever given that impression. It is true that as a so-called professional Christian I am, to some extent, paid to pray, but I have never felt that there was a secret to discover which would guarantee answers, end the mystery, or remove the struggle of prayer.'

Rosemary's reaction was one of surprise. My answer, apparently, was not as predictable as I imagined. Surprise is very often the reaction of people when they get close enough to the so-called experts and discover just how it is. As I have often told people in such circumstances, I am not a bishop who is trying hard to be a human being, but a human being who is trying hard to be a bishop. A human being with all the weaknesses and frailties of humanness. The further I go in the Christian life the greater becomes my awareness of just how little I know and how much more there is to learn about God and, indeed, about prayer. This fact has come home to me with renewed force in recent days from within an ordinary domestic situation.

One of the pleasures and pains of retirement is getting rid of all the junk you have accumulated over the years. My wife and I have lived in 14 different houses and carried with us, from our first to our thirteenth home, various bits and pieces, including visual aids for children's talks, just in case we would need them! But an industrial skip, over the contents of which, with just a touch of nostalgia, I pronounced the last rites, has put an end to all that. We now travel lighter and are none the worse for it.

But one collection proved to be the most painful to dump. No, it wasn't innately valuable. It had no sentimental charm, quite the reverse; indeed, it was part of me that I was dumping. Holding on to it filled me with guilt. Letting go of it meant admitting failure though, in a strange way, brought me freedom. It was the motley collection of failed systems of prayer, meditation, and secrets of spiritual growth that I had purchased, devised, concocted and tried to use over the years of my life and ministry. There was a sophistication about some of them which must have attracted me at the time but now appalled me. I had started all of them with enthusiasm and with the best of motives but, sinner that I am, I had completed none of them.

In one sense I was sad to see them go, for they reminded me of my foolishness and pride and served to keep me more humble than I might otherwise have been. In another sense the banishing of them to the skip represented the gradual discovery, over the years, that simplicity rather than sophistication is the hallmark of the life of prayer.

Device or relationship

Simplicity as opposed to sophistication also marked the difference between George's reaction to unanswered prayer and that of Rosemary. As I talked with them, on separate occasions, it became clear that though they shared the same contradiction of unanswered prayer their reaction to it was totally different. Rosemary saw it as something to be overcome by using the right kind of manipulative formula, whereas George, though it tried his faith, had learned to accept it even though he couldn't understand it. The former saw prayer in terms of trying to prise open the hands of a somewhat reluctant God. The latter saw it as a relationship which, like most relationships based on love, has moments of pain and perplexity.

I had some empathy with Rosemary. She was fairly young in the faith and reminded me a little of what I was like in the early days of my own spiritual journey. I still blush when I recall some of the things I demanded of God in those days. It could be described charitably as youthful enthusiasm. Honesty, however, requires me to describe it as immaturity bordering on arrogance, linked to a misunderstanding of the nature of both God and prayer. The remarkable thing is that God in his wisdom and patience seemed to say yes more often than he said no. But then I also had more patience with the precociousness of my children when they were very young than I did when they grew older!

Once or twice during my walks I encountered a similar precociousness on the part of adults in this matter of unanswered prayer. To put it bluntly, they weren't prepared to take no for an answer. They had what they called a 'name it and claim it' formula. They believed in battering on the doors of heaven or, perhaps, taking an acetylene torch to the brass, in their desire to see the way of God, as they saw it, prosper. I admire such determination and faith. It is often a rebuke to the lukewarm, nominal, and vague faith which is prevalent in some quarters. But to be frank, it is an attitude which I find difficult to emulate. It may have as much to do with temperament as with holiness. In my mind it raises questions about the nature of God and our relationship to him.

However, the majority of those who raised the question of prayer during my pastoral walks saw it, as George did, in terms of relationship. It was something very personal, it was based on love and trust and, far from being static, it grew towards maturity. Elsie's words summed it up for most people. She was an alert, active and prayerful pensioner who, without trying, communicated the joyfulness about her relationship with God. 'Bishop Roy,' she said, as we walked along a dales footpath, 'I don't take God for granted, after all he is God and I'm only one of his creatures. But I believe that he loves me and wants the best for me; isn't that why he sent Jesus? So I place my confidence in him, tell him what is on my heart, and leave the rest to him. I may get mixed up or confused sometimes in the way I pray for things and people but I think he sorts it all out up there. And even if I don't get an answer then that too must be for the best.'

Elsie's philosophy of prayer might be rather simplistic for some but it is certainly not without its wisdom and theological depth. It revealed a faith based on her knowledge of the character of God as seen in Jesus and, in its own way, acknowledged the sovereignty of God. It saw prayer as a relationship of love, admitted her inability always to get her motives right, and placed unshakable trust in God to do the right thing – even if that meant withholding an answer. It was a very positive approach to prayer, even unanswered prayer.

The answering Father

It was an approach I tried to commend to Rosemary, and indeed to others who appeared to be getting hung up on the negative rather than the positive aspects of prayer. God is the God of the open hand rather than the closed fist. He is revealed in Scripture, and in the life and work of Jesus, as a generous God, one whose love, as Elsie so rightly pointed out, wants the very best for us. This creator God, who invites us to call him Father, desires to receive and answer the prayers of his children.

He is revealed in the teaching of Jesus as 'the answering Father'. How else can we understand those remarkable words of Jesus in the Sermon on the Mount in connection with prayer? 'Ask, and it will be given you; search, and you will find; knock, and the door will be opened for you. For everyone who asks receives, and everyone who searches finds, and for everyone who knocks, the door will be opened' (Matthew 7.7–9).

Here, clearly, is a massive encouragement to prayer

and, indeed, to persistence in prayer. But that persistence is not motivated by God's apparent reluctance to answer, quite the reverse. It springs from a conviction about his lavish generosity. The key words in this passage are 'how much more'. If earthly fathers respond to the requests of their children by giving them good things rather than bad, 'how much more will your Father in heaven give good things to those who ask him!' (Matthew 7.11).

John in his Gospel record gives us similar encouragement from the lips of Jesus when he said, 'I will do whatever you ask in my name, so that the Father may be glorified in the Son. If in my name you ask me for anything, I will do it' (John 14.13–14). And again, 'Very truly, I tell you, if you ask anything of the Father in my name, he will give it to you . . . Ask and you will receive, so that your joy may be complete' (John 16.23–24). God is not only interested in receiving our prayers, he also appears eager to answer them.

Yet, if we are honest, it is not always as simple or as satisfying as it sounds. There are disappointments. Some people appear to do better than others when it comes to getting what they ask for. As Christmas approaches each year I inwardly groan at the prospect of receiving the customary flood of round robin letters. I love my friends and acquaintances, but can it always be true that their children seem to be doing much better than mine? Can it always be true that God seems to be answering their prayers more than mine? Can it be true that God appears to be more interested in answering prayers about GCSE grades and piano lessons than he does about floods and famine across the world? I believe we must be careful lest our claims about the power of prayer in our domestic concerns inadvertently portray God as too small.

I believe in a God who answers prayer. At the same time I am conscious that we must be mature and sensitive in the way we express that faith. If we as Christians, unintentionally, give the impression that we have a hotline to God and that, therefore, in comparison to us, everyone else is disconnected from his love and generosity, we may give a false picture of God and distort the gospel. Was it not while we were yet sinners, and disconnected, that Christ died for us?

A wise proviso

It is because God showed us his character and his great sacrificial love for us in Christ that the teaching of Jesus on prayer is so very important. It is through his words and example that we know that God's door is open, his name is Father and his heart is love. It is through him we know that, within this loving relationship, we can bring anything to God in prayer. It is through the example of Jesus that we learn that every prayer request we make to God must carry this rider, 'Your will be done'. The pattern was set in Gethsemane, as he wrestled with the great contradiction of what God had sent him to do and what his humanity desired. 'My Father, if it is possible, let this cup pass from me; yet not what I want but what you want' (Matthew 26.39).

These words of Jesus are a necessary corrective to an

unhealthy and selfish triumphalism in prayer which narrows everything down to 'me and mine' and ignores the larger picture. Jesus refused to ignore the large picture. Even the encouraging words from the Sermon on the Mount quoted above, despite their unlimited scope, need not imply that God will answer every request as we would wish. They have a wider import than asking God to do some things that we are capable of doing for ourselves. Within their context the words point to the basic principle of God's comprehensive and faithful care of his children not only in the present age but also in the coming kingdom of God.

There is a wider context also surrounding prayers offered and answered in the name of Jesus as mentioned above in John 14 and 16. To pray in the name of Jesus is much more than simply using a formula. To pray in Jesus' name implies that we are in union with Jesus. If we are in union with Jesus and Jesus is in union with the Father, then our requests will be granted.

But there's more to it than that. I believe that in John 14.13 Jesus lifts our eyes beyond the petty requests of life. He calls us to focus on those requests of such a nature that when they are granted, the Father 'is glorified in the Son'. They are requests pertinent to the Christian life and to the continuation of the work by which Jesus glorified the Father during his ministry (John 17.4). These are the prayers which never go unanswered; indeed, when Jesus prayed this sort of prayer, the words were hardly out of his mouth before the answer was given. 'Father,' he prayed, when visited by the Greeks during his final trip to Jerusalem, 'glorify your name.' 'Then a voice came from heaven, "I have glorified it, and I will glorify it again"' (John 12.28).

If our prayers appear to be unanswered perhaps the first question we need to ask is to what extent, if any, were they motivated by a desire to see God glorified and his kingdom brought nearer? There are, of course, specific reasons for unanswered prayer, namely selfishness or opposition to the ways of God within our lives. It was the Psalmist who, when giving thanks for an answer to his prayers, was perceptive and honest enough to say, 'If I had cherished sin in my heart the Lord would not have listened' (Psalm 66.18, NIV). In other words there are reasons why, on occasions, God appears to turn a deaf ear.

A great orchestra

In an unguarded moment, at the beginning of my last pastoral walk, I let slip that I had a secret desire to conduct a great orchestra. The bush telegraph was soon in operation and by the time I reached St Agatha's my hidden desire became a reality. After a wonderful patronal festival service at which I preached and a military band had played I was unexpectedly handed a baton, placed in front of the band and invited to get on with it. Wow! I had a wonderful time. The musicians had been primed, of course, and however I waved the baton, and it was fairly unpredictable I can tell you, they played the right tune and at the proper tempo – and we all managed to finish together. Oh, I did feel good. It was a night to remember.

But my desire to conduct an orchestra was not only prompted by my love for music but also because it has always provided me with a meaningful illustration of the place of prayer. Early in my Christian life I had discovered the wonderful truth contained in the letter to the Hebrews, namely that 'Jesus ever lives to make intercession for us' (Hebrews 7.25). In other words, his prayer never ceases and as we chip in with our little effort it is caught up with his and presented unceasingly before God. Like the varied instruments of an orchestra under its conductor, the multitude of prayerful voices from across the world and across the ages unite with Christ in a harmonious and continuing offering of praise and prayer to the Father.

It is this thought that helps me in the apparent contradiction of unanswered prayer. If my prayer is genuinely offered in the name of Jesus I believe it is caught up with his and offered to the Father. There is no possibility of it being left unanswered.

And yet, the mystery remains. When Jesus hung upon the cross there was a brokenness not only in his body but also in his relationship with his Father. 'My God, my God, why have you forsaken me?' (Mark 15.34). There is no answer to that cry of dereliction. Nevertheless, Jesus maintains faith in a Father who, by any human standards, had let him down, let him suffer and let him die. Out of the darkness of forsakenness that surrounded him there came from his lips this amazing confession of trust in the faithfulness of God his Father – 'Father, into your hands I commend my spirit' (Luke 23.46). His confidence was not misplaced, for three days later God raised him from the dead.

Living with the contradiction of belief in a God who encourages but doesn't always answer prayer, and certainly not in the way we expect, becomes possible and ultimately profitable if, like Jesus, we have confidence in the character of a God whose faithfulness is sure and whose name is love.

7

Where is God when it hurts?

Walking along the river bank on a mild and sunny spring morning it was easy to believe that 'God was in his heaven and all was well with the world'. The weather had been fine for days and many folk from local churches had joined me on my pastoral journey each day. All had opted to walk except Jane. She had no such option for she was a victim of a degenerative disease and sat in a wheelchair pushed by her husband Andrew. It was a gentle reminder that all is not well with the world and that suffering creates a contradiction in the lives of many.

But in Jane's case you wouldn't have known it. She was like a breath of fresh air, fully determined to enjoy every minute of the walk along the riverside. Known by many and admired by all for her courage in the face of adversity, she revealed no obvious self-pity. Instead, she thoroughly enjoyed the company of others and showed a lively interest in their concerns. To walk and talk with

Jane and Andrew was a delight. It provided me with one of those life-enhancing encounters that gives a new dimension to life and helps to put mundane anxieties into perspective.

An impression gained

It also reinforced an impression, whether true or false, that I have gained over the years, namely, that those who experience personal suffering are not usually the first to complain to God about it. Very often it is their family or friends who do so on their behalf. At least three other people during that morning's walk, for instance, got alongside me to point out the unfairness of Jane's affliction. 'What is God playing at?' said one. 'Why is it always the good people who suffer?' asked another. The third contented herself with saying, 'I don't know how Jane and Andrew keep so cheerful in the circumstances.'

The circumstances certainly were difficult. Jane's career in the world of education had been a promising one but it had come to an abrupt end with a sharp deterioration in her condition. With two children approaching their teens and a husband with a demanding profession, the structures of family life seemed to be collapsing around her. However, her faith was deep and firm, her family was supportive, and the local church offered regular and practical pastoral care. Such understanding and help enabled her to play a limited but significant part in the life of the church as well as exercise her responsibilities as a wife and mother. Her

Christian witness within the neighbourhood was a powerful one.

Nevertheless, despite her faith, the understanding of her family and the support of the Christian community, she did have times of darkness, despair and doubt. As the needs of her two children increased so also did the force of her inner contradictions. It wasn't always easy to reconcile her conviction about the love of God with her failing health and the family pressures associated with it. Her public face of serenity often hid a private face of anguish. Anger, frustration, uncertainty and tears became a painful part of family life.

I have heard it said that faith is the courage and ability to live with doubt. Jane proved that saying to be true. With the practical and loving help of her family and friends her faith not only survived the times of doubt and despair but seemed to grow stronger as a result. Certainly, few of us who walked with Jane and Andrew by the riverside that day will ever forget the enriching experience. When I said goodbye to them at the end of the walk I am sure they were totally unaware of the effect and influence they had had upon us all that day.

No easy answers

But not all can cope with suffering in the way that Jane and Andrew seemed to do. Sometimes fear threatens to drive out faith. At other times anger gains the upper hand and bitterness destroys any prospect of a calm and prayerful acceptance of suffering. I have also known a few instances where suffering has been met with an unhealthy triumphalism of faith that has claimed, even demanded, healing. Such an attitude hasn't always produced a happy outcome. On occasion the lack of healing, and the subsequent deterioration of the illness, has caused great distress to the person and family concerned, to say nothing of the shock waves that have rocked the community of faith as a result.

It is always an inspiration to witness people like Jane apparently triumphing over suffering, but I have never found triumphalism an appropriate reaction to it. Of course, there have been times when the only appropriate response to a remarkable recovery from illness has been unstinted praise and thanksgiving to God. More often than not, however, there has been a feeling of helplessness, humility and tears in the face of unrelieved suffering. God gave us tear ducts and Jesus showed us how and when to use them. Despite the fact that he would shortly afterwards raise his friend Lazarus from the grave, Jesus wept in the presence of suffering, grief and death (John 11.35). I can't help but feel that Jesus' tears may have revealed something of the contradiction that the Lord of life experienced in the presence of death.

Helplessness and tears were part of my own reaction to suffering on two occasions during my walks. Rarely a day went past without at least one person asking me to pray for a relative or close friend who was seriously or terminally ill. On two occasions, however, I was asked to make a detour from the planned route in order to visit someone who was dying.

The first was to a young husband suffering from

cancer. It was heartbreaking to stand by the bedside with his wife. She was courageously keeping up an air of competence and control. At the same time she was wondering how she was going to cope with life in general, and three young children in particular, when he had gone. It was not possible to keep the tears back as I gave a blessing to David and commended him and his family to the care of a loving Father. I would be dishonest if I did not confess to a contradiction within myself as I thought of the loving Father and saw the withered frame of a human father lying before me. Would a loving Father not have given him back to his loving wife and children?

The second was during a tour of a local hospital. I always made a point of visiting hospitals en route during my walks in order to offer encouragement to the staff and express appreciation for the work they did. While talking to the staff in a special care unit for children the Sister asked me if I would speak with a young couple whose child had been horribly burned in a domestic accident and wasn't going to recover. Inwardly my heart sank and a feeling of dreadful inadequacy swept over me. As the father of five healthy children and seven grandchildren could I, with integrity, say anything helpful in such circumstances?

But I knew from experience that words are rarely needed and seldom helpful on such occasions. In the numbness of grief words, however well-meaning, cannot always be heard. It was a time for silence, for standing alongside and weeping with those who weep, for prayerfully embracing a dying child within the love of

God. We must be wary of trying to take away the pain of tragedy and death either by false comfort or easy explanation. We cannot take it away and, perhaps, we ought not to try. But we can share it without pretending that we know or understand the depth of their pain. That young couple had to walk a terrible road. It was possible for me, if only for a short time, to walk along with them. It seemed better to walk in silence.

A day of victory and tragedy

Walking, mainly in silence, alongside the suffering and bereaved, was a lesson I learnt when, as Bishop of Bradford, I was involved in the aftermath of the dreadful fire disaster at the Bradford City Football Club in May 1985. It was meant to be a day of victory, to celebrate the winning of the third division and promotion to the second division of the football league. Instead, it became a day of tragedy as fire, accidentally started at the base of the stand, quickly and fiercely engulfed the whole structure and resulted in the death of 56 people. They had left home for an afternoon's entertainment and never returned.

The tragedy traumatized the whole city. There was a spontaneous outpouring of grief which needed to be expressed in a communal way and, following a brief announcement on local radio, it seemed that the whole community came together in the cathedral for that purpose. In silence and in prayer they declared their symbolic solidarity and sympathy with the suffering and bereaved. Words were few and sensitively chosen, but the silences were profound. A multicultural and multifaith community was united in grief.

In the weeks and months that followed the work of healing began, and still continues, for such horrendous events leave their mark on whole families and communities for decades, as people in Lockerbie and Dunblane can testify. There was one aspect of that event which certainly left its mark on me because it took place in my home.

Several weeks after the disaster an open-air memorial service was held in the football stadium. Because the families of the bereaved were somewhat uncertain and fearful about such a service, especially as it was being televised, it seemed right to invite them to my home the week before to help prepare them for it. As there were about 150 coming I asked a few other ministers to be present to help in case people needed pastoral care or counselling. I needn't have bothered. The families, in a quite remarkable way, cared for and ministered to each other. I found small groups of them all over our large house sharing and sympathizing with each other. A woman who had lost a son in the fire found comfort and strength from another who had lost a husband and two sons. Lives were slowly being rebuilt. Gradually healing was taking place within families. Suffering families were helping suffering families to cope with their pain.

This held deep biblical and Christian significance for me, for one of the descriptions of Jesus that I like best is that of 'the wounded healer'. Certainly those who themselves had endured suffering and bereavement as a result of the fire disaster had an integrity and authenticity, based on experience, which I and others could not match. Heart spoke to heart. It is a gentle reminder that we must approach suffering in any shape or form with tenderness, compassion and a humility which is ready to listen before we speak. I learnt this the hard way on two occasions when I was a patient in hospital. The first was humorous, the second more serious.

On the first occasion I was suffering from recalcitrant kidney stones and was in absolute agony. In the midst of my pain I received two visitors within five minutes. They didn't assuage my pain but they certainly tried my patience. They were both clergymen! One was a Baptist, the other an Anglican. Having heard that I was in hospital where they served as chaplains they got to my bedside fairly quickly and, having greeted me, began to have a conversation with each other across the bed. For the life of me I can't remember what they said to each other, being somewhat preoccupied with what was happening in my kidneys.

However, even in my pain I began to recognize the tell-tale signs as they each began to wonder whether or not they ought to pray with a fellow parson. Having decided that it would be a good thing, they then had a brief demarcation dispute as to who should do the praying. Their conversation went something like this. The Anglican said to his colleague, 'I think it would be good to pray with our brother, will you say a prayer?' 'Oh', replied his colleague, 'Since you are the Anglican chaplain I think you ought to pray, after all I'm only a Baptist.' 'Well', said the Anglican chaplain with great gusto, 'I've never heard a Baptist pray before, it would be a joy if you prayed.' By this time I'd had enough and, through the waves of pain that afflicted me, I heard myself saying, 'Brothers, push off, and I'll pray for myself.'

The second occasion was in a London hospital where I was recovering from a major heart attack. I was visited by another chaplain, a woman. She had done her homework before she reached my bed and knew that I had suffered permanent damage to my heart. She said little, other than to give me a blessing and promise to bring me Holy Communion next morning. Before leaving she gave me a little picture card on which was a verse from the psalms. In the light of my heart condition, and my uncertainties as to whether or not my ministry as a diocesan bishop was finished, it was the most apt word I could have received: 'A wounded heart, O God, you will not despise' (Psalm 51.17b, NEB).

These personal memories illustrate in different ways the need for sensitivity in the use of words when confronted with suffering in others. They also indicate that there is value in a sensitive silence.

Why does God allow it?

There are always those, of course, who when faced with human suffering and disaster choose to speak before they listen. It is understandable. They are deeply distressed by the suffering inflicted on others through disease or disaster and so angered by it that they cannot keep silent. Instead, they criticize God for his silence on the matter and for his apparent failure to prevent it happening. It is a common reaction. It is also declared by many to be a barrier to their belief in God. I believe that such people are sincere in holding this view though, to be honest, if there is no God, and suffering still remains a dominant fact of life, the problem of suffering becomes even greater and more insoluble.

Andrew, the husband of Jane, with whose story I began this chapter, made a similar point when I talked with him during a visit to his parish church some weeks after we had walked by the riverside. He picked up on the few negative comments that people had made about God in connection with Jane's illness. As we talked it became clear that the faith which enabled both him and Jane to cope with the contradictions of life was a very thoughtful one. He appreciated people's concern for Jane and understood the good intentions of some of his friends in demanding that God should do something about her illness. At the same time he was unhappy about the concept of the kind of interventionist God that some were suggesting. He felt that it portrayed a God who acted in a totally arbitrary fashion, choosing whom he would help and whom he would ignore.

He had sympathy, and some emotional identification, with those people who, in disaster situations like Bradford, Lockerbie and Dunblane, questioned the existence of a God who was all-powerful and all-loving, yet failed or refused to prevent such tragedies. But Andrew held a different viewpoint. He believed that the logical conclusion to such a view would turn God into a kind of puppet-master, endlessly pulling strings all over the universe. The actions of such a God would make human life meaningless, destroy human dignity and rob us of freedom and moral choice.

I believe Andrew was right. Parents who controlled their child's every emotion, who anticipated their every need and manipulated their every action, would stunt any possibility of mature and moral development and make spontaneous love virtually impossible. God does not behave in such a possessive and manipulative manner. He doesn't obliterate our personalities or crowd out our space for growth. He allows a creative balance between care on the one hand and freedom on the other.

The Bible reveals God as one who does take sides, who cares passionately enough to get involved. He is on the side of goodness against evil. He is on the side of those who need justice and against those who withhold it. And, as the Virgin Mary said in her Magnificat,

> 'He has shown strength with his arm;
> he has scattered the proud in the thoughts of their hearts.
> He has brought down the powerful from their thrones,
> and lifted up the lowly;
> he has filled the hungry with good things,
> and sent the rich away empty.'
>
> (Luke 1.51–53)

But God is also revealed as a God who hides himself

(Isaiah 45.15), and whose ways, on occasions, are shrouded in darkness and whose purposes for us are surrounded by uncertainty. We look for his clear guidance and find none. We desire an answer to our prayers and are met with silence.

We worship a God who loves us so much that he came to dwell with us in humility at Bethlehem, a God who loves us so much that he allows us space to take decisions, make mistakes and even doubt him, in order that we may come to a maturer faith. He is a God who by sending his Son to die for us revealed that he is on our side, yet who trusts us to follow even when the darkness of suffering and despair hides him from our eyes. He is a God who doesn't smother us with care or treat us as puppets on a string. Because he loves us, he takes the risk of setting us free and gives us his Spirit to help us to use that freedom to be our true selves.

Even Creation, which was the gift of his love, has an inbuilt degree of freedom to be its true self and not the 'play-dough' of a manipulative master. God didn't, as it were, create a world with the brakes on. Creation was a risk. All acts of creative love involve risk and creation is no exception. Things go wrong and result in natural disasters. People get hurt, God's failure to intervene is criticized and an explanation is demanded.

Where is God when it hurts?

Before replying to that question from a Christian perspective I think there is value in listening to a Jewish perspective. During a televised documentary recording his first visit to Auschwitz, site of one of the death camps during the Holocaust, Jonathan Sachs, the Chief Rabbi, said, 'I am often asked, "Where was God at Auschwitz?" I don't know. But it is the wrong question. The real question is, "Where was humanity at Auschwitz?" God didn't say he would stop us harming one another. He gave us a moral code, commandments engraved on stone, which taught us how to stop ourselves. So the real question is not, "Where was God when we called to him, but where were we when he called to us?"'

The Chief Rabbi's words are a powerful and pertinent reminder that some of the world's suffering is self-inflicted and calls for us to confront injustice and defend human rights whatever the personal cost.

It is this thought of personal cost that begins to answer the question, 'Where is God when it hurts?' The Christian answer, based on the Scriptures, to that question, centres on the cross of our Lord Jesus Christ. Through the death of his Son, God entered into the suffering of humankind. Writing to the young church at Corinth, St Paul made this amazing statement about God's involvement at the cross: 'God was in Christ, reconciling the world to himself' (2 Corinthians 5.19). God was no mere spectator of the crucifixion. He identified with and endured the suffering it entailed. The silence that greeted the cry of dereliction from the lips of Jesus, 'My God, my God, why have you forsaken me', does not mean that God is absent – quite the reverse. It means that he is present, that the darkness is also affecting him and that the crucifixion is also being experienced by him. The cross declares that God is not immune to suffering nor does he stand outside the darkness. He is right there in the midst of it. Perhaps the darkness is a corporate symbol of the Son's dying and the Father's grief at his death or, as Jürgen Moltmann, the German theologian, has said, 'The Fatherlessness of the Son is matched by the Sonlessness of the Father' (Moltmann, 1973, p. 243). Where is God when it hurts? He is on the cross and in the darkness, for he is the crucified God.

Of course, the cross doesn't let God 'off the hook' in connection with the world's suffering. The contradiction is still there. The mystery remains. But at least he shares the contradiction and experiences the pain with us.

When you think of it, the only visible body which God presented to the world was that of his Son who suffered pain and death on a cross. That is reflected in the Church's central act of worship where bread is broken and wine is outpoured as symbols of the broken body and outpoured blood of the Son of God at Calvary. Thus week by week we are reminded of the fact that God, far from abandoning us in our suffering, declares through the cross that he is on our side.

It is for this reason that, over the years, I have adopted the practice, when visiting the seriously ill, of giving them a small wooden cross that fits snugly into the palm of the hand. When darkness engulfs them, when pain makes it difficult to concentrate, when words fail to penetrate or soothe the mind, the feel of the wooden cross in the hand is a reminder that God is on their side and is with them in their suffering.

It carries with it another message, of course. It is a symbol of the love which, having embraced suffering, even unto death, on the cross, transformed it through the resurrection, thus declaring that suffering, evil and death do not have the last word. That no matter how strong our inner contradictions and uncertainties might be, the cross and resurrection are God's guarantee that he will not abandon us. We are held in his love, which never fails. We are sharers in his resurrection life, which never ends.

8

Walking the edge holding the centre

Walking the edge holding the centre was not only the theme of my first pastoral walk as Bishop of Southwark, it also contains the clue to living purposefully with contradictions.

It has several layers of meaning. It indicated, for instance, that I was walking right round the 130 mile circumference of an area that covered most of south London and some of east Surrey, calling in at the 77 churches that were on the boundary of the diocese. At the same time it declared that while doing that I would also be in touch with the 300 other churches in the centre of the diocese by way of a personal card, hand-written and posted to them at the end of each day's walk. Blisters on the fingers as well as blisters on the toes were a daily possibility.

But there was also an image of mission built into the theme. The Church is called to be a partner with God in his mission to the world and bishops are called to be leaders of mission. It is a task which requires the

Church to take the message of God's love, which must first be embodied in its own life, to the edges of society. The Church is not to be content with speaking to, or engaging with, its own members only. It is called to move out to the edges of society, to grapple with complex moral and ethical issues, to confront injustice, to challenge unbelief, and to witness to the incredible generosity of God towards all people. It is a privileged calling and one which carries great responsibility.

At the same time the Church is to remember that its primary task is to worship God. At the centre of its life and mission is the daily, weekly, corporate encounter with the living God in worship and particularly in the Eucharist. What the Bible calls 'the breaking of the bread' is meant to be an event of such life-transforming power and influence as to motivate the members of the local church for mission to the community in which they are set. How can we, with integrity, offer to others a life-changing gospel, if that same gospel is not motivating, transforming and renewing our own lives week by week?

The rhythm of mission

But undergirding all this, and providing the pattern for living creatively with contradictions, is the example of Jesus. There was a symbolic rhythm about his life and work that was both impressive and effective. There were intimate times of worship and prayer with his Father before he moved into, and towards the edges of, the society surrounding him (see Mark 1.35). There were times of withdrawal and quietness and there were periods of intense pressure with hardly a moment to call his own. There was a continuing movement in towards God for prayer and out towards society in service and mission. It is an example that was not only pertinent to my pastoral walks but also to the continuing life of faith of us all.

This is why, I believe, Jesus included a lesson on this rhythm of life in the training of his disciples (Mark 6.31). He took them aside for periods of rest and renewal before sending them out to engage in mission activity like healing and preaching and serving. These periods of prayer and instruction at the centre, as it were, equipped them for ministry on the edges. 'I am sending you out like lambs into the midst of wolves', was his charge to them (Luke 10.3). Clearly, reaching out to the margins and functioning on the edge, where the church meets and engages with society, is a risky business. But it is where Jesus often found himself as he kept company with the outcasts and sinners. It was while walking on the edges of tradition and prejudice in society that he encountered so much opposition from the religious authorities of his day (Luke 15.1–2).

Those of us, therefore, who feel called to follow him today must not be surprised to find ourselves experiencing some of the uncertainty, vulnerability and inner contradiction that accompanies a life of discipleship on the edges of life in the world. How important it is, therefore, for us to be closely linked with the corporate life of worship, prayer and fellowship within the local church. Walking the edge may be a risky occupation but it can become purposeful and secure if we are holding, or being held and supported by, the centre. It was holding and being held by the centre that enabled Jesus to walk the edge and engage in mission so effectively. His relationship with his Father and the Spirit, within the communion of persons known as the Holy Trinity, formed a centre of love in which he, uniquely, and all God's children, are held. It was a point I found myself emphasizing over and over again as I tried to encourage the faith of the thousands of people who took part in my pastoral walks.

Circumstances and contradictions

To a large extent the contradictions with which so many of them lived were caused by the fact that the circumstances of life demanded that they walk the edge, while their faith also required them to hold the centre. The vast majority of them were committed to Christ through their local church. But that commitment was being lived out in a society which, by and large, was not sympathetic to the gospel. So day by day they were being faced with new and sometimes destructive challenges to their faith and practice.

Jean, for instance, was having her faith stretched to the limit in her work in a large secondary school. There had been a time when, as a teacher, she had enjoyed taking worship assemblies. Now she was terrified. She believed in the power of the gospel of love but such was the secular influence, and the power of ridicule towards faith in her school, that she was having, in modern parlance, to 'hang in there' as a Christian. She was having to live with the contradiction of a belief in the power of the gospel and the fact that it seemed to cut no ice in her school.

John, on the other hand, was having to apply his Christian standards and values in a harsh economic climate and in a highly competitive market. Others were not so scrupulous and were prepared to cut corners and engage in dubious practices in their fight for survival. But even John's Christlike compassion for people had to be placed alongside the need for his firm to survive a period of intense economic pressure. It meant he had to make hundreds of people redundant so that many more could remain in employment. His action, though necessary, distressed him immensely and caused him great heart-searching.

As for Patricia, she was just deeply disappointed that she hadn't made as much progress in the faith as she desired. As a churchwarden in her local parish she was totally committed to a life of faith, but the care of her large family had consumed most of her time and energy. She was sad that only one of her five children was a practising Christian and three others had broken marriages. She lived with the anxiety that if she had been a better Christian things might have been different.

For Jean, John and Patricia, and thousands like them, the inner contradictions that they live with on a daily basis are not produced by a lack of faith nor by a compromised Christian commitment. Rather, they are the result of living in the real world where faith and experience often come into conflict. They come about because the desire to follow Christian principles and practice is not always rewarded by a sense of achievement. All too frequently the achievement which Christian people desire and for which they pray is hindered by circumstances entirely beyond their control. Far from being an indication of the absence of faith, such contradictions and the feelings of failure or frustration that go with them are often signs of faith's reality and vitality. It was genuine faith that made Jean 'hang in there' in the world of education. It was courageous faith that helped John to make right choices rather than cut corners. It was persistent faith that enabled Patricia to remain committed to her church and her family over against so many domestic discouragements.

We're getting there

Such inner contradictions are also part and parcel of the Christian's journey of faith. Like any other journey it has its share of ups and downs, sunshine and shadow, conflicting demands and wrong turnings. It is when we forget that we are on a journey of faith, rather than certainty, that inner contradictions and inconsistencies can sometimes disturb and deflect us from our chosen pathway. Conversely, it is our vision of the goal or destination towards which we are travelling that makes the journey worthwhile and keeps us going. It is our awareness of the centre, the communion of love in which we are held, that not only makes the journey possible but also gives significance and purpose to the difficulties encountered on the way.

I remember vividly, as a young Christian, being bowled over with wonder and excitement at the new status that had been given to me in Christ. Passages of the Bible, like Ephesians 1.3–14, enthralled me. I found their description of the scope of God's grace absolutely breathtaking. The truth that God was not just a generous God, but that he had 'lavished' that grace and generosity on me and others, was mind-blowing. So much so, that I recall going for long solitary walks and singing aloud the praises of God for the privilege of being called to follow Jesus. It is a practice I have maintained into old age, though the length of the walks and the quality of breath available for singing have somewhat diminished.

However, the further I have gone on the Christian journey, the more I have come to realize that though God has lavished great riches of grace, forgiveness and love upon us, he has also left us room and given us encouragement to make progress on the journey and to grow in the faith. Indeed, that is part of the message of the letter to the Ephesians. Yes, we are called to this amazing privilege of being in Christ, members of his body, and sharers with others in the life of God. But that is not the end of the journey, it is only the beginning. There is a goal to be achieved, a destination to be reached. And though, like the old British Rail slogan, 'We're getting there', we certainly have not yet arrived.

That's why the writer to the Ephesians, having graphically reminded his readers what they once were in sin, and what they now are in Christ (Ephesians 2.10), went on to advise and instruct them how they were to become what they are (Ephesians 4—6). In other words, along with their brothers and sisters in Christ, they were to grow in grace, truth and love in order to become the kind of persons God had called them to be, namely, 'filled with all the fullness of God' (Ephesians 3.19).

Stepping stones or pitfalls?

This sense of journey, achievement and destination, and some of the inner contradictions that go with it, are graphically demonstrated in the writings of Paul. There is, for instance, his famous 'thorn in the flesh' experience, recorded in 2 Corinthians 12. Paul, apparently, was in danger of getting above himself because of a rather special revelation he had been given by God. God, therefore, gave him a 'thorn in the flesh' to keep him humble and, to some extent, to teach him a lesson. We are not told specifically what this thorn consisted of. But whatever it was, Paul saw it as a hindrance to his work and asked God on three separate occasions to remove it. God refused. Instead he supplied the grace for Paul to live with 'this sharp splinter that had got under his skin': 'My grace is sufficient for you, for power is made perfect in weakness.'

It would certainly be stretching credibility to describe Paul's thorn as an inner contradiction. Nevertheless, I am sure its presence was a constant reminder of the contradiction, perhaps paradox, that 'Whenever I am weak, then I am strong' (see 2 Corinthians 12.7–11). Paul was discovering what multitudes have discovered across the centuries, including many of those who accompanied me on my walks, that inner contradictions are often the growing pains of the life of faith. Prayer requests refused, suffering apparently imposed, and frustrations inflicted upon us by the church, can become the raw material for growth towards maturity in Christ. As long as we see them as purposeful and creative they become as stepping stones on the journey of faith. If, however, we get them out of perspective, and lose our sense of holding and being held by the centre, they can become pitfalls that disturb our peace and undermine our journey.

Raw material for growth

Paul's classic statement about this journey of faith is found in the third chapter of his letter to the Philippians. He is under no illusion that he has finished the journey, achieved his goal or reached his destination. Despite the spiritual maturity of this mighty servant of the gospel, he declares that he has not yet arrived, but is pressing on to lay hold of that for which God laid hold on him in that famous encounter on the Damascus road. I believe that one of the great contradictions of Paul's life and work, apart from the many other frustrations and conflicts he encountered, resulted from that transforming experience.

Throughout his great missionary endeavour Paul carried two great burdens, the burden of failure and the burden of success. The failure consisted in the fact that in attempting to serve God he had persecuted the Church. The success consisted in his great missionary work as the Apostle to the Gentiles. In his lonely and depressed moments, and there are some hints in the Bible that he had both, I am sure the sadness of past failure vied with the joy of past success in his thoughts. Perhaps that is why he said, 'forgetting those things that lie behind and straining forward to what lies ahead, I press on towards the goal' (Philippians 3.12–16). In his obedient pursuit of the call of God he refused to be paralysed by past failure or impeded by past achievement. He lived creatively with the contradiction not by pretending it didn't exist, but by consciously setting it behind him and fixing his eyes on the goal, the prize, the destination, namely, the 'heavenly call of God in Christ Jesus'.

What is meant by 'heavenly call'? What is the prize for which Paul keeps running and which he is sure he will receive? Though various suggestions have been made, I believe that the context encourages us to see the prize as Christ. To know Christ fully and completely was the prize for which he had been striving ever since his encounter with Christ on the Damascus road. He knew, however, that such knowledge and such completeness would only come at the end of his earthly life when he saw Christ face to face. This is the meaning of his words in 1 Corinthians 13.12: 'For now we see in a mirror, dimly, but then we will see face to face. Now I know only in part; then I will know fully, even as I have been fully known.'

Paul, knowing that the prize awaited him, was not prepared, as it were, to sit back and let it happen. Despite frustrations, opposition and imprisonment, he pressed on. In the face of outer conflicts and inner contradictions, he kept his eye on the goal and continued striving and running for the prize who was Christ, fully and completely known. Even the experience and frustration of being in prison he saw as advantageous for the gospel (Philippians 1.12) – he had a captive audience for his teaching and preaching! He had the vision to view every aspect of the race he was running, the difficulties as well as the delights, as the raw material that would contribute to his ultimate joy of obtaining the prize of seeing and knowing and being like Christ (1 John 3.2).

The old mangle

It is this thought of seeing and knowing and becoming like Christ which Paul seems to anticipate in those wonderful words in 2 Corinthians 3.18: 'And all of us, with unveiled faces, seeing the glory of the Lord as though reflected in a mirror, are being transformed into the same image from one degree of glory to another, for this comes from the Lord, the Spirit.'

I never read these words without being reminded of the old mangle my mother had when I was a child, long before washing machines and spin-dryers were commonplace. In those days I was fascinated to stand and watch the water cascading into a tin bath underneath, as she turned the handle of the mangle and pressed various items of clothing, that she had washed by hand, between the twin rollers. Many years later, when producing the parish magazine before word processors came on the scene, I saw something similar. It was used for a different purpose and powered by electricity. It was called an electronic stencil-cutter and had two large rollers just like our old mangle. The original image, drawn on a sheet of paper, was placed on the top roller and a blank stencil was placed on the bottom roller. With the press of a button the rollers turned with great speed and the image of the original was scanned and imprinted line by line upon the blank stencil that was exposed to it on the roller below. When the image was complete I was able to use the new stencil to reproduce a mirror image, as it were, on the pages of hundreds of parish magazines.

Completing the task

All illustrations have their limitations and this one is no exception, but over the years it has been a source of joy and encouragement to me not only in trying to understand Paul's words in 2 Corinthians 3.18 but also in living with the contradictions of life. Exposure to the life and character of Jesus Christ, as revealed in Scripture through the enabling and creative work of his Holy Spirit, results in our lives being changed from one degree of glory to another.

It doesn't happen all at once, however. It takes a lifetime and more to complete. Gradually, the characteristics of Christ, who is the perfect image of the person God intends us to be, are imprinted on us. It feels sometimes, as we take one step forward and two steps back in the process, as if it will never be completed. But such feelings, though real, are incorrect. As Paul said to his readers, 'I am confident of this, that the one who began a good work among you will bring it to completion' (Philippians 1.6). God always completes the work he begins. He always keeps his promises. He is worthy of our trust.

The contradictions we have to live with are challenging, but they are indicative that we are God's children on the way to our destiny in Christ. They are the evidence of our dual citizenship of earth and heaven, that though our future is secure, our journey towards it takes us through an uncertain and imperfect world. They are the proof that while we are already enjoying the riches we have in Christ, we are not yet in possession of our full inheritance. They are the signs that though we may be walking the edge we are still holding and being held by the centre – that divine community of love we call Father, Son and Holy Spirit.

Therefore, using such contradictions as incentives rather than hindrances, let us not just walk but, in the words of Hebrews 12.1–2, 'run with perseverance the race that is set before us, looking to Jesus the pioneer and perfecter of our faith'.

References

Auden, W. H., *The Orators*, Faber, 1932

Davie, Grace, *Religion in Britain Since 1945*, Blackwell, 1994

Horne, Alastair, *Macmillan*, Volume 2, Macmillan, 1989

Issues in Human Sexuality, House of Bishops' Report, Church House Publishing, 1991

Moltmann, Jürgen, *The Crucified God*, SCM, 1973

Muir, Frank, *A Kentish Lad*, Bantam, 1997

Sachs, Jonathan, *Roshannah*, TV documentary

Ward, H. and J. Wild, *Christian Quotation Collection*, Lion, 1997